The Enlightened Gardener

A NOVEL BY
Sydney Banks

INTERNATIONAL HUMAN RELATIONS CONSULTANTS, INC.

© 2001 by Sydney Banks
First printed in 2001   10 9 8 7 6 5 4 3 2 1
Printed in Canada

Published by
INTERNATIONAL HUMAN RELATIONS CONSULTANTS, INC.

This novel is a work of fiction. All names, characters and incidents are the
product of the author's imagination. Any resemblance to actual events or
persons, living or dead, is entirely coincidental.

Distributed by Lone Pine Publishing

10145 - 81 Avenue   1901 Raymond Ave. SW, Suite C
Edmonton, AB T6E 1W9   Renton, WA 98055
Canada   USA

Website: www.lonepinepublishing.com

Canadian Cataloguing in Publication Data

Banks, Sydney
   The enlightened gardener

ISBN 1-55105-298-9 (bound) -- ISBN 1-55105-243-1 (pbk.)

   I. Title.
PS8553.A57E54 2001 C813'.54   C00-911289-8
PR9199.3.B367E54 2001

Editorial Director: Nancy Foulds
Project Editor: Randy Williams
Production Manager: Jody Reekie
Layout & Production: Arlana Anderson-Hale, Monica Triska
Cover Design: Robert Weidemann

We acknowledge the financial support of the Government of Canada
through the Book Publishing Industry Development Program (BPIDP) for
our publishing activities.

PC: P1

Table of Contents

A Note to the Reader

In this simple book, the author endeavors
to explain in his own unique way the connection
between our spiritual nature and our
psychological nature.

Chapter 1

A Conference
in England

*W*e seldom have any clue that a life-changing event is waiting in the wings. The experience that was to forever change my life and career, the lives of three close colleagues, and, some would say, the entire field of psychology, began with a chance conversation. A year later, in the spring of 1968, that experience resumed with an unportentous transatlantic flight and the events that followed.

As a practicing psychologist, I have always looked forward with great anticipation to learning what is new in my field. To this end, I was on my way from my Denver home to a conference in England in early June. My wife, Norma, had stayed behind to treat herself and her mother to a music festival they had been looking forward to for months. Traveling with me were Dr. Tom Newman, who also practiced in Denver; Dr. Peter Richards, a long-time friend who worked in a clinic in New Jersey; and last, but not least, my very dear friend, Dr. Janet Maxwell, who worked mainly as a marriage counselor in Phoenix.

Janet, a slim, attractive woman in her late 20s, was a willowy 5'6". Probably her most striking feature was her gorgeous auburn hair, which tumbled in a shining cascade to her waist. Apart from her physical beauty, she was then, and still remains, something of a free spirit, blessed with a wonderful sense of humor and an IQ that appears to outshine those of most of her peers.

Tom, on the other hand, was definitely not a happy person. A man in his late 50s, medium height, starting to add a few extra pounds around the middle but still distinguished looking, Tom was rarely seen smiling in public and was considered to be as stubborn as a mule. This stubborn streak, along with his over-indulgence in alcohol, was perceived by his friends and colleagues as the main obstacle to his leading a successful, happy life.

Peter Richards was trim and fit, standing about 6'2" and, like Janet, in his late 20s. His long, fair hair hung down to his shoulders, framing an intelligent face with smiling blue eyes. Peter, a very enthusiastic young man with great pride in his profession, wanted nothing more than to help people.

Our flight was quite pleasant. We spent the first few hours catching up on each other's doings before the conversations turned to more general topics. The whole world appeared to be in turmoil. We debated the value of demonstrators trying to stop the war in Vietnam before it escalated beyond anyone's control and whether or not their efforts would have any significant effect. We discussed the sad news of presidential candidate Robert Kennedy's assassination, a topic weighing heavily on most everyone's mind. On a lighter note, we touched upon the latest shenanigans of The Animals, a rock music group that Peter particularly enjoyed. Then, after an unexpectedly good airline meal, Tom shuffled papers while Peter and Janet settled down to read and I absent-mindedly thumbed through a journal. In truth, I found myself musing on the unexpected turns my life had taken.

We arrived at Heathrow International Airport, cleared customs without event, and rented a car. Since I was the only one who had any experience piloting a car on the left side of the road, I was designated to drive. After a night's rest in London, we followed the motorway north and west towards the little town of Bourton-on-the-Water, and from there drove four miles south to the conference site. The trip went fairly smoothly, with a minimum number of hair-raising encounters with round-abouts and fast-moving British traffic.

Upon our arrival, my three colleagues were pleasantly surprised to see that the Old Swan Inn was a magnificent Tudor hotel surrounded by immaculate lawn and manicured gardens. It looked like something straight out of a Thackeray novel. The small-paned, leaded glass windows and the prolific, deep green ivy that covered the stonework were indicators of the hotel's age. It was in amazing condition for a building which I had been told was built in 1684.

Entering the small hotel lobby, we mingled with some old friends and introduced ourselves to others. After registering, we agreed to check out our assigned rooms and meet in the lobby about 20 minutes later.

My accommodations were just as I remembered them from my first visit, a little over a year earlier, when I had attended a similar conference and stayed in the very same room. I stretched out on the bed and thought back to that time. I started to recall the unusual chain of events that had occurred and how a chance encounter with a mystical gardener had enhanced my understanding of myself, and life in general, beyond my wildest dreams. As of yet, I hadn't told my colleagues about my new findings—or that those findings had nothing to do with the actual conference I had attended last year.

When I suggested to my friends that they should come with me to England, I didn't mention that it was not so much for the conference itself, but to speak with this uncommon gardener. I felt it would be better for them to meet the old gardener for themselves than for me try to tell them what little I remembered of my conversations with him. I felt quite inadequate to describe to my colleagues the fascinating and informative meetings that had taken place on my last visit to the Old Swan Inn.

As open-minded as I felt, little did I know just how profound and mystical an experience my second encounter with the gardener would be.

My colleagues and I met in the lobby as planned. We were eagerly looking forward to hearing some of the British and European doctors speak on their various new findings. "They're opening the conference room," Janet announced. "We'd better move if we expect to get good seats." The four of us made our way into the meeting room, where a Dr. Samuel Smith opened the conference and introduced the afternoon's speakers. Some presented various new techniques and theories that appeared to be positive and to show great promise. On a less hopeful note, the second speaker, a therapist from France, talked about the frustrations suffered by practitioners who see the same patients repeatedly readmitted to hospitals. Also on the agenda were discussions regarding the identification of a few new mental illnesses.

After the day's speakers had finished Tom, Janet, Peter and I went for coffee. Afterwards, we decided to stretch our legs with a stroll through the gardens. As we discussed the various topics that had been presented, I allowed that I had often thought that if this trend of constantly finding new mental illnesses didn't stop, there soon wouldn't be any "sane" people left—and that made me feel very insecure.

"It's interesting you should think that way, too," Janet said. "I often feel the same hopelessness you describe. At times I wonder if I shouldn't have taken my father's advice and joined him in his hardware business."

We all laughed when Tom quipped, "Perhaps we *all* should have gone into your father's hardware business."

Stifling a chuckle, I observed, "Human psychology has an aspect of intangibility, unlike physics or mathematics, which are pure sciences. The trouble is, we have no universal constants to work with."

"Depressing, isn't it?" Peter replied. "You would think with all the books available to us, there would be more answers. Between the wise pioneers of the past and the scholars and researchers of today, you'd think someone would have found the healing answers we seek."

Shrugging off such high-minded talk, Tom turned to me and said, "I hear through the grapevine that your clinic is doing very well and is expanding. What's your secret, Eric? What kind of techniques are you using these days to bring you all this success?"

Holding back a smile, I hesitated for a few seconds before answering Tom's question. "If I told you, I'm sure you wouldn't believe me," I said finally. "As for techniques such as role playing, I don't use them any more."

Tom was incredulous. "Why not?"

"Because, as far as I'm concerned, techniques are great for tennis and other physical activities, but in my workshops, I find they are seldom of any value whatsoever."

"What do you do if you don't use any techniques?" Tom sneered.

"What I do in my sessions these days is strictly dialogue," I replied softly. "Like I said, I'm not quite sure you'd believe me if I told you."

"Why wouldn't we believe what you're doing?" Janet wanted to know. "Is it that weird?" She nudged me gently to let me know she was teasing, but I could sense she was genuinely intrigued.

"No, it's not weird, Janet, but it has nothing to do with what we were taught in grad school. Apart from that, it was someone completely outside the field that put me onto it."

"What do you mean, it was someone outside our field?" Peter asked.

I hesitated for a few seconds, then thought to myself, here goes nothing. "Well, actually," I said, "the person who put me onto this totally new approach was the old gardener who takes care of these hotel grounds."

Tom exhaled sharply. "Are you expecting us to believe that an old gardener imparted some great wisdom that brought you success in your practice? Surely you must be joking!"

"No, I'm not joking at all. I'm entirely serious. The last major conference I attended was held in this very hotel, and that's when I talked with the gardener who worked here. What I learned from him not only helped me change my own life, but aided me in my practice."

"What's the big deal about talking to a gardener?" asked Janet. "And what on earth does that have to do with helping your patients get better?"

"Before you dismiss what I'm saying, Janet, let me assure you that this man is no ordinary gardener."

Smiling condescendingly, Tom immediately cut in. "Okay, so he's a *great* gardener. Now what exactly did this mysterious fellow tell you that was so inspiring?"

"Okay! But I know you'll think I'm crazy," I muttered as I stopped at one of the many garden benches.

"For goodness sake, Eric, we're all friends here," Peter said with a chuckle. "Get on with it—we'll believe you."

"Maybe," Janet giggled.

I sat on the bench and studied the expressions of my three friends—Peter's features appearing open and curious, Janet's gently teasing, Tom's set almost in a scowl—and knew it was now or never. "Okay," I began. "It was just over a year ago..."

Chapter 2

My Introduction to the Gardener

I had been sitting on this very bench, feeling quite despondent about the way my life was going. Apart from that, I'd been thinking seriously about having to retire in only 15 years and the thought of it honestly scared the hell out of me. To complete my mood, everything that day had gone wrong.

Then I noticed an old gray-haired fellow planting some flowers. He stood maybe 5'7" and wore an old but respectable sports jacket with work pants muddied at the knees. He appeared to be absolutely absorbed in his work, but suddenly seemed aware of my watching him. Glancing up, the gardener asked me in a friendly, curious tone if I was one of the doctors attending the conference.

"Yes I am," I replied, though not with much enthusiasm.

"How's it going? Are you learning much?"

"A little."

"What do you talk about in your meetings?" the gardener asked.

"Oh, we share our experiences and try to help each other by discussing various new approaches and techniques. Nothing terribly exciting, I'm afraid."

"Sounds interesting," the gardener replied sincerely. "Do you enjoy helping others?"

"Very much so. That's why I became a therapist in the first place. I must admit to having started out with great expectations about someday being able to truly help people who are suffering, but now I sometimes find myself wondering if the stress it creates for me is worth it." The gardener was looking at me with a quizzical expression. "Don't get me wrong," I explained. "I've helped many clients throughout my career, and such successes were very gratifying to me. Yet there are times when I have to wonder if the entire world is going crazy."

The gardener, sensing my dejected state, immediately put his work down and sat beside me.

Extending my hand, I introduced myself. "Eric James."

The old man wiped his hand on his pant leg, then, as he shook my hand, he said, "Andy Miller. Call me Andy."

"Pleased to meet you, Andy. You've done a beautiful job with the hotel gardens. Did you design the grounds?"

The gardener smiled. "Lad, these grounds were designed before your grandfather was born. I just have the honor of being their temporary caretaker."

"You must get a lot of satisfaction from your work," I commented.

With a twinkle in his eye, he said, "I love every day I spend here. There's something about helping plants grow that has always appealed to me. I take it you don't get much joy from what you do?"

"At the moment, I can't say I do," I admitted.

The old gardener looked me straight in the eye and said, "Why not think about some of the successes you've had in your work?" With an infectious smile he said, "That should help you feel good. After all, there's no sense being unhappy when you can be happy, now is there?"

Then, with a wink, the gardener left. His parting words made me think of the old saying my mother had often quoted: "Just as well to be happy as sad." No sooner had I thought those words than I found myself smiling. All the heavy negative feelings I had been experiencing suddenly started to diminish.

When I look back now, I realize that it felt like someone had lifted a 10-ton load off my shoulders. I remember thinking to myself, "What a nice man. He talks with such light-heartedness and common sense."

By happy coincidence, the gardener and I bumped into each other the following day. For the longest time we discussed the various species of flowers and shrubs on the hotel grounds. I remember his saying something to the effect that we had similar jobs, explaining that as a gardener his job was to rid the garden of unwanted weeds, while as a therapist it was my job to help my clients rid their minds of unwanted thoughts that were harmful to their mental well-being.

"That certainly is a unique way of putting it, but I must admit it makes perfect sense," I chuckled.

Then the old gardener suddenly changed the course of the conversation, asking me, "What are you hoping to find at this conference?"

His penetrating question took me by surprise and it was a little while before I responded. "To be truthful, I don't really know," I answered. "I certainly would like to find more understanding that would help me in my work. To date, I think I've read almost everything written—and traveled many miles—searching for some kind of answer. As a matter of fact, a friend and I once went on a six-month trek to India and Nepal, hoping to find someone who could share some wisdom. We had some wonderful adventures and thoroughly enjoyed our vacation, apart from the fact that we both suffered intermittently with dysentery. But as for wisdom, we found very little, if any at all. I think I can honestly say that we both arrived back in the States just as ignorant as when we left."

Andy smiled and said, "I guess ignorance must be one of the most common afflictions there is. I've often suffered from it myself."

I laughed at Andy's words, then started to tell him more about my travels throughout India and

Asia. I mentioned that my friend and I had met and heard many very wise teachers on our travels, but unfortunately, for some reason, none of their wisdom rubbed off on us.

The gardener cleared his throat and said, "Have you ever considered that the answers you seek are not in India or Nepal but right where you stand?"

"What do you mean, right where I stand?"

"You know, Dr. James, one of the greatest misconceptions in this world is that wisdom is found outside oneself. Didn't anyone on your Asian journey ever tell you to look *within* for the wisdom you sought?"

"As a matter of fact, yes. I was told that quite a few times. But you have to understand, Andy, that when I was in India and Nepal I went to see special teachers, people who are very wise."

"Wiser than you?" the gardener asked?

"Heavens, yes! Much wiser than I am. That's why people from all over the world go to see these teachers—they are exceptionally enlightened individuals."

"Are you sure you're not selling yourself short?" Andy asked. "What if I told you that you are just as wise as any of the teachers you met in India—or any other place—but just don't realize it?"

His answer surprised me and I found myself short of words to reply. "I wish I were," I said.

There was a mysterious quality to this gardener that I couldn't define, a confidence in his utterances that astonished me and at the same time made me feel very insecure. The more we talked, the more I realized this man was no fool, and certainly no everyday gardener.

I explained to him that I'd been lucky enough throughout my years of education to have the privilege of studying with some of the best professors in our field.

"Perhaps you did," he replied. "And for this you should be grateful. But this doesn't mean there aren't deeper answers to the questions you now perceive regarding you personal life and your profession."

"What you say may be true, but where does one find such answers? Believe me, this kind of knowledge has eluded many a better man than I."

The old gardener smiled, and to my absolute amazement he said, "Maybe *I* know a little something that can help you."

It seemed quite obvious to me that the old gardener had no comprehension of what he was talking about, and it tickled my sense of humor that he actually believed he knew "a little something" that could help me to find some answers.

I didn't want to appear rude, so I hid my smile and asked Andy how he could help me. The answer he gave set me back on my heels; it certainly wasn't what I'd expected, and I'll never forget what he said.

"Has anyone ever suggested to you that the secret to healthy psychological functioning is woven from three spiritual gifts which are the fiber of all human realities?"

I had never heard such a statement. I sat astounded. "What do you mean, three spiritual gifts?" I blurted. "I'm afraid I have no idea what you're talking about!"

The old gardener picked up his shovel and started to dig a hole for his next flower. But then he stopped, rested his chin on the shovel handle, and calmly began to explain.

"The way I see it, there are three gifts, and they are:

> The power and the gift of
> *Universal Mind,*
> The power and the gift of
> *Universal Consciousness,*
> and the power and the gift of
> *Universal Thought.*"

That answer was, to say the least, out of the realm of what I had been taught in school. So I told the gardener, with a certain amount of pride, that my profession is one of the most complex fields imaginable.

Ignoring my interruption, Andy asked me if I ever talked to my patients about their thoughts being directly linked to their problems.

"Well, of course," I replied. "But only in a very general way. As I just said, my profession is one of the most complex there is, dealing with people's behavior, emotions and the conditions of their lives. I'm afraid merely talking about their thoughts wouldn't help my clients too much."

"How do you know if you have never tried?" he responded.

He took me off guard with that question. Then, in his very quiet English voice, the gardener suggested that there was more to the power of *Thought* than I was realizing.

When I asked him exactly what he meant by such a statement, he said, "*Mind*, combined with the *power of Thought* and the *power of Consciousness*, are the determinants we use to direct ourselves through life. We can choose to use them wisely or unwisely. If we use them unwisely, our lives can become a long series of bewildering periods when we feel utterly lost. On the other hand, if we use them wisely, we will experience more contented lives."

Again, I told the gardener I doubted that such a theory would make much difference in my life, or in the lives of my clients.

Andy looked at me, smiled and said, "I'm not really interested in your clients' problems. After all, I'm not a therapist. I think their therapy is better left to you. I'm much more interested in why you didn't find any wisdom in India."

I was flabbergasted. "I thought you said the truth I was looking for was not to be found in India."

Smiling, the old gardener said, "It was there

when you were there; now it's here in England with you. Don't forget, Eric,

> *Wherever you go,*
> *Truth is with you always."*

Before I could ask him what he meant by this puzzling reply, the old gardener stood up, lifted the handles of his wheelbarrow, and trundled away—leaving me to wonder what on earth he was talking about.

And that was the last I saw of Andy the gardener, although I must confess that the concepts he shared with me that day continued to resonate in my mind throughout the rest of the conference—and beyond.

Chapter 3

Mrs. Taylor's Story

*W*hen I had finished telling the story of my first visit to the Old Swan Inn, I found myself looking into the startled, uncomprehending faces of Janet, Tom and Peter. After an awkward pause, I attempted to gauge their reactions by saying, "I thought to myself how ridiculous it was for some old gardener with absolutely no training in the field to come out with such outlandish statements."

"That *is* quite a concept," Janet remarked, "especially coming from an old gardener."

"That's how I felt, too, at the time," I replied. "But believe me, Janet, this guy is different. To be honest with you, there's a mystical quality about him that sometimes unsettles me enormously. A good part of the time we talked I had the strongest feeling that he knew something I didn't, and that feeling made me quite insecure and vulnerable around him. Later that same day, after lunch, I went to hear a Doctor Martin's presentation on schizophrenia. But it all sounded just like the same old lectures I'd heard a thousand times before. Apart from that, the inevitable arguments broke out as practitioners from various approaches adamantly swore that their approach was better than the others. At one point I felt like screaming and walking out of the meeting hall."

"I know *that* feeling," Peter chuckled.

"That evening I lay in bed, unable to sleep, thinking about the whole situation. Then the old gardener's words came back to me: 'The answer you seek is contained in and created by the three very precious spiritual gifts of *Universal Mind, Universal Consciousness* and *Universal Thought.*' During my schooling I'd had very little training on any of these three subjects. Certainly consciousness was rarely mentioned, and thought was believed to have little or nothing to do with mental stability."

"If I remember correctly," I continued, "mind was defined in all of my university courses as a synonym for the brain. Consciousness was defined as a state; a person was either conscious or unconscious. Thought was talked about in our psychology courses, but in a very limited way, as a blanket word for the content of cognition, and it had very little to do with psychological nature. Now here was this gardener trying to tell me that thought was part of the solution to my dilemma. To say the least, I thought the old fellow's words were oversimplified, so I dismissed the whole conversation, feeling it was absolutely ludicrous. Yet, things the old gardener said kept going around and around in my head. Try as I might, I couldn't erase them from my mind. I pondered over, rejected, reconsidered, and again discarded his words to the extent that I began to wonder if such a conversation had even taken place. Let's face it, how many people have any of you met who actually talk in such a bizarre fashion?"

Peter laughed and replied, "Lots—and most of them are patients."

Janet, Peter, and even Tom were anxious to hear more about the gardener. Janet especially had a curious look about her, as if she were very deep in thought. Finally she asked, "What was it about this gardener that got through to you?"

Knowing Janet's intellectual capabilities—and her pithy sense of humor—I didn't want her to think I had lost some of my marbles, so I continued my story quite hesitantly.

"Now this is the way it was, and I'm only telling you what actually happened. On the flight home, I couldn't shake off some of the gardener's statements and my mind was in turmoil. I had a very difficult time accepting the way he spoke with such certainty about his theories and beliefs. As a practicing therapist, I couldn't imagine allowing myself to get upset over some old gardener's opinions. Finally, I completely dismissed his words, deciding he was just a nice old crackpot who liked to talk.

"About one week later, at an office meeting, I

was informed that I would be getting a patient who had been undergoing therapy for 10 years, someone who had been shifted from one therapist to another with little or no success. To make things even worse, this woman had been under psychiatric care involving heavy medication for the previous two years, again with no positive results. I couldn't help but think, 'Why me? Why am I getting stuck with such a difficult case?'

"The next morning my receptionist ushered Mrs. Taylor into my office. She was a woman in her mid-30s, married with two children, but her appearance was that of a woman at least 10 years older. Her face was drawn tight and lined with stress; hers was a classic case of depression.

"During her first two intensive sessions with me, I tried all the techniques I knew for breaking through to a depressed person, but I made no progress. She seemed to feel worse and worse. During the third session, I was at my wit's end. Just looking at her, it was obvious the poor woman was in mental agony, and I desperately wanted to help alleviate at least some of her suffering.

"Suddenly the words of the old gardener came to mind, and for some inexplicable reason I felt a tingling sensation throughout my entire body. I heard myself saying, in sheer desperation: 'Mrs. Taylor, don't you think it may be your own negative thoughts that are creating some of your problems? Why don't you try to stop *thinking* about all your troubles. These are *your* thoughts,

25

and you have the power to think whatever you want. Perhaps having a more positive attitude towards life would help you greatly.'

"I have no idea why I said these words. They just popped out of my mouth, seemingly of their own volition.

"Janet, you'll never believe this. To my absolute astonishment, the woman looked at me, stood up with tears in her eyes and said, 'My God, you're right! My own thoughts *are* creating much of my unhappiness.' Then she kept repeating over and over again how wonderful it was to finally see that she was unknowingly causing a lot of her own problems. As she talked, she threw her arms around my neck and began to sob uncontrollably. I was so disarmed by her response that I didn't know what to say. I hadn't said anything that would create such a reaction, at least not that I was aware of. As she gradually regained control, she kept saying through her tears, 'It's such a relief, I'm so relieved.'

"I asked her if she could possibly tell me what I had said to her that was getting her so excited. To my utter amazement, she explained to me that she had just realized she had been holding old grudges and ill feelings against her father for many years. She said she had suddenly recognized that her habit of judging people was connected with her anger toward her father, and that her negative feelings had spilled over to her poor husband and children. She asked again and again, 'Why didn't anyone tell me before that my *own thoughts* were responsible for most of my anxieties and mental stress?'

"I sat behind my desk, astonished by her behavior, wondering what had happened. I just couldn't put my finger on anything I had said that would account for her insight and breakthrough.

"Totally bewildered, I asked her again what I had said that was creating such a reaction. The second time she explained it in the following way: 'Don't you remember? You just explained to me that my *own thoughts* have been creating a great many of my problems.'

"Here I was, the therapist, and I didn't know what my own client was talking about. Immediately, I thought about the old gardener and wondered if it was possible for him to know something that I hadn't been taught in grad school. It certainly appeared so. I tell you, chills ran up my spine as I tried to ascertain just what was happening."

"I'm getting chills right now," Janet said. "I'm all goosebumps."

Tom asked scornfully, "Are you trying to tell us that just because your client heard you say that some of her problems were created from her thoughts, she is under the illusion that she has found the answer to a dysfunctional life pattern that was established during her childhood?"

"Yes, but it's *not* an illusion," I countered. "The amazing part of all this is that the visit we're talking about took place nearly a year ago, and to date Mrs. Taylor is still a very happy, loving person, with absolutely none of her old symptoms. She is off her medication and even looks 10 years younger than she did the day I first saw her."

"Unbelievable," Tom scoffed. "I've never seen such a spontaneous recovery in all my years of practice. You were lucky, that's all. It must have been a one in a million fluke to help a client with such an obvious technique. Have you ever tried it again?"

"Tom, it's not a technique," I said quietly. "As I've already said, I no longer believe in techniques. And, in answer to your question, yes! I've successfully helped many of my patients by talking about how their own thoughts are responsible for their perception of life."

With his usual penetrating intellectual astuteness, Peter asked, "If what you say is correct, why hasn't the field taught this theory?"

I could only shrug. "I don't know, Peter."

"As a therapist, I find what you are saying ridiculous and very difficult to believe," Tom fumed.

"Believe it or not, Tom, I'm telling you the truth."

Janet chimed in, "Do you really believe this is the reason you have been having such success in your practice?"

"Most definitely. Even after so many years in the field, it wasn't until I listened to the old gardener that I finally started to realize how our minds and thoughts—working together—observe and relate to the realities in which we live. To date I haven't figured out how it all works, but the results in my clients are indisputable."

"I've never heard such a preposterous story," Tom protested. "Surely with all the brilliant professors and researchers throughout the world, we would have heard about such a simple theory if it actually worked."

Janet was intently studying my face. "Eric, you really *do* believe what you're saying, don't you?"

"Yes I do, Janet. I'm absolutely serious."

Still skeptical, Peter couldn't help sounding a bit intrigued. "I wonder if that old gardener of yours still works at this hotel?"

"I don't know," I replied. "But I hope so. For more than a year, I've been looking forward to meeting and talking with him again."

"If I didn't know you better," Janet chuckled, "I would think you've had one too many to drink."

"Think what you like, Janet. But never before have I seen such results. I've seen couples who were ready for divorce heal their relationships practically before my eyes. Months later they tell me how wonderful their lives and marriages have become, just because they realized that many of their problems were directly created from their own *innocently misguided thoughts*. I honestly believe I've stumbled onto something that is well worth pursuing further."

"I knew your practice had been expanding," Peter said. "To be honest with you, I couldn't figure out why. This whole story is intriguing. Tell us more about what it is that you think you've found."

At that, Tom abruptly stood up and snapped, "Personally, I think you're all talking a bunch of utter nonsense!" He then stormed away, obviously disturbed by the entire conversation.

"Whew!" Peter whispered. "I wonder what's bothering Tom? I've never seen him so upset."

Janet quietly explained to us that Tom had been going through a lot lately. His divorce had just been finalized and he'd been drinking to excess. In fact, his partner had threatened that if Tom didn't do something about his alcohol problem, he would have to leave their practice. "Apart from that," she concluded, "well, you know Tom. He quite often suffers from a severe case of righteous indignation, especially when he's had a few drinks."

Peter shook his head. "No wonder he's so touchy lately. I didn't know the poor guy was going through so much."

Changing the subject back to what the gardener had said about *Mind* and *Thought*, Janet recalled that one of her professors in college had almost burst a blood vessel when one of her classmates had asked him whether there was a correlation between our thoughts and our behavior. "If I remember correctly, the professor actually informed her that if she continued to ask such ridiculous questions, she would undoubtedly fail the course. If he were here now, that professor would react like Tom and dismiss everything you have told us as total nonsense. Come to think of it, Tom and my professor share the same negative outlook and behavior in life."

Laughing, Peter suggested, "It must be their *thoughts* that are holding them back." He then advised us not to take my gardener friend too seriously. "Honestly, Eric," he laughed, "you're describing the kind of experiences that I'd expect to find written up in 'Ripley's Believe It or Not.'"

"I don't know, Peter," Janet mused. "A similar idea has come into my mind from time to time, but I've never actually formulated it into a theory—nor have I ever heard of it in practice before now."

"If we were to take a closer look at the situation," I suggested to Peter and Janet, "we would see that most of our research to date has been descriptive. We have observed people acting in certain ways and then labeled these behaviors. We often assumed the cause of their problems was located in their past or in their genetic make-up. As far as I know, we haven't looked for the deeper source of all these distinct behaviors in the realm of *thought*."

"Hmmm," Peter said. "Let's assume, just for a moment, that the old gardener is correct in saying that all our personal realities are derived from the way we think. This would mean that many of the entities we talk about in therapy, such as the ego, the id and so forth, would also be made up entirely from our personal thinking. If this were so, it would revolutionize many of the diagnoses we therapists now assign to people."

Janet exclaimed, "Wow! This discussion really has the wheels in my head spinning. But if people could transcend their past more easily, it certainly would provide more hope for a lot of our patients. The big question is, What is it exactly that helps your patients change their thinking?"

"I'm not sure," I admitted. "But I definitely think it's time to look for that old gardener again!"

Chapter 4

My Colleagues Meet the Gardener

*T*he following day, I asked the concierge if an old gardener named Andy was still employed at the hotel.

"Oh, yes! He still works here," she said. "As a matter of fact, I just saw him a few minutes ago."

"Thank you," I replied. "That's all I wanted to know."

Later that afternoon, my colleagues and I were taking a break from the various lectures. Some of the speakers had been truly boring, and our heads were swimming with seemingly endless statistics and details from case studies.

Peter suggested that the four of us go out into the garden to get a breath of fresh air and try to sweep out the cobwebs that had gathered while we attended the lectures. As we strolled through the grounds, he asked, "What did you think of that last speaker and her theories on maintaining a healthy marriage?"

"I couldn't believe she was for real," Janet

said. "Sometimes I wonder where they dig up these speakers. She appeared absolutely lifeless, and her ideas were as stale as last week's bread. Did you know she has been divorced three times and is now going through her fourth? It is inconceivable to me that a person with her background can presume to speak about healthy marriages. I sure wouldn't want any advice from her about my marriage if it were in trouble. As a matter of fact, she scares me. You know, at times I wonder why, with our training, many of us can't get hold of our own lives or marriages. How can we possibly be expected to help others with their lives if we can't help ourselves?"

Tom chuckled joylessly. "Think of it this way, Janet," he said. "If you went to see that speaker for help, you would be getting an expert on marriage, divorce and the wedding ceremony—all rolled into one appointment." Janet, however, failed to see the funny side of Tom's sarcastic remark, and she let him know it in no uncertain terms.

I told my friends that I had decided to seek out the gardener with the intent of having a little chat with him. Janet asked if she could tag along, saying that she found my story intriguing; the others came along, claiming they had nothing better to do. We asked a passing staff member if she knew the gardener's whereabouts, and she gave us directions to the fountain, saying she thought Andy was working there.

Sure enough, we found the old gardener working on his lawn near the fountain. On approaching him I reintroduced myself, then introduced the others. "You probably don't remember me, Andy," I elaborated, "but a little over a year ago I met and talked with you while I was attending a conference here."

"Oh, yes! I remember you," the gardener said with a smile. "You're the doctor from Denver."

"Man! You have a good memory. I never thought you'd remember me. I've been telling my associates about our conversations, when you told me what I should be looking for is the connection between *Mind, Consciousness* and *Thought*. Do you remember? You suggested that I should look very closely and see how they are connected to the way we see life and react to it?"

"Can't say that I do," Andy replied. "But it certainly sounds like me."

I continued, my words pouring out in an excited torrent, "I also remember that you said something to the effect that our thoughts have a great bearing on the quality of our lives. I'm not saying I understand what you were talking about—I barely remember much of our conversation! But I do remember you said something like, 'Hanging on to old negative memories is psychological suicide.'"

"I'm afraid, doctor, you have a better memory than I do," the old gardener replied. "I can't remember saying those exact words, but it's definitely something I might say."

I told him that the gist of our conversations had stayed with me, and that his suggestions had changed the way I looked at life and the way I talked to my clients. "To be truthful with you, Andy, at first it was baffling to me when some of my patients started to change simply because I had talked about their minds and thoughts having a direct link to their problems. Then, as time went by, I myself gradually started to understand how our thoughts definitely *do* have a direct link to our outlook on life. But to this day, I still have many nagging, unanswered questions about how it works."

I then related Mrs. Taylor's remarkable story and asked him if such results made any sense to him.

Peter, Tom and I sat in silence, while Janet gently splashed the waters of the fountain, waiting for his reply.

Finally the old gardener said, "It's fine weather for this time of year. You're lucky—quite often it rains cats and dogs in June. But I guess we can't complain about good weather, now can we?" Picking a flower from the border by the pool, the gardener observed that there was a similarity between a flower and one's mind, saying, "If a flower gets good care and lots of love, it should grow strong and healthy. On the other hand, if you give a flower too much manure, it will be destroyed. Same with your mind—if you give it too much manure, you will destroy it."

Completely baffled by his response, I said, "I don't quite understand the correlation between giving a flower too much manure and nurturing your mind."

Andy winked. "You think about it for a while, Eric. I'm sure it will come to you." Both Peter and Janet smiled—seemingly they got the picture.

Still grinning at his own witticism, the old gardener casually remarked that many people fail to realize that life is a spiritual journey.

We were all somewhat surprised by the gardener's statement because it seemed to introduce an abrupt change in the direction of the conversation. Finally, Tom asked the gardener to explain what he meant.

The old gardener fumbled in his pocket, looking for his spectacles, while we sat in anticipation, wondering how he would reply. "Darn things! I can never remember where I put them. What was the question again?"

Impatiently, Tom repeated, "What do you mean by 'life is a spiritual journey'?"

"Oh, I remember now," Andy said. "I left them in my jacket pocket."

Janet didn't even try to hide her amusement at Tom's obvious frustration as we all waited for the old gardener to reply to his question.

Finally Andy said, "Right! Now then, what I meant to say is,

> *Life is an illusionary, spiritual*
> *journey confined*
> *within the boundaries of time,*
> *space and matter."*

"Wait a minute," Peter complained. "Now you really have me confused. What has all this got to do with psychology?"

"Everything!" The gardener answered. "Don't you know? This world we live in is merely a *psychological phenomenon*."

Both Janet and I burst into peals of laughter at the bewildered look on Peter's face as he tried to grasp the meaning behind the old gardener's succinct reply. Tom merely looked away and shook his head in disgust.

"I'm afraid I just don't follow your line of reasoning," Peter finally responded.

Andy looked straight into Peter's eyes. "Are you sure you want me to try to explain my ideas?" he asked. "After all, I'm untrained in your field and I don't want to cause any ill feelings because of our different opinions."

"Yes, I really *do* want to hear more," Peter answered. "You triggered my curiosity when you said that the world as we know it is a psychological phenomenon. What on earth did you mean?"

The gardener moved closer to the fountain and leaned against its edge. "The way I see it, young man, we were given three special gifts to assist us through life. They are *Universal Mind*, which is the source of all intelligence; *Universal Consciousness*, which allows us to be aware of our existence; and *Universal Thought*, which guides us through the world we live in as free-thinking agents.

"Together, these three components are the

golden threads from which all human experience is woven. No one can exist without them; they are the necessary components through which we acknowledge life. Without any one of these three principles, life would not exist for any human being. They are the psychological trinity of all human functioning."

There was a long silence as the four of us tried to absorb the gardener's answer.

Andy scratched his head for a little while. "Let me put it another way," he said. "It is my belief that life is a cosmic stage. To enable us to play our part in this universal drama, we were given the three special gifts I just mentioned. But keep in mind, these three gifts are completely neutral. *It is what you as a thinker do with them that is important.*"

Still a bit puzzled, I said, "Are you saying that if we can understand the correlation between *Universal Mind*, *Universal Consciousness* and *Universal Thought*, this understanding will bring us some of the answers that we seek?"

With a nod of his head, and another smile beginning to play at the corners of his mouth, Andy simply replied, "Yes."

Peter countered, "Surely it's not that simple! Many learned people throughout time have searched in vain for such answers. Have you any idea of the enormous task in finding just *one* thing that will help in our field? Do you realize the amount of research required?"

After a long silence, Andy said, "As I already

told you, I know very little of how you therapists function—and I'm afraid I lack the memory and intelligence to understand or retain all of your terminology. But, to satisfy an old man's curiosity, tell me something—anything—that you can be aware of without any one of these three gifts."

Tom immediately retorted, "What about our emotions?"

"No," Andy replied. "To have an emotion, one must have *Thought* to create the emotion and *Consciousness* to be aware of it."

"What about our moods?" Peter asked. "Are you saying moods don't create our thoughts?"

"On the contrary," answered Andy. "It is the very opposite! Our thoughts *allow* our moods to exist."

Janet had a startled look on her face. She asked Andy, "What do you consider to be the role of thought in our lives?"

"The way I see it, Luv,

> *Universal Thought is the mystical*
> *paint brush,*
> *and the reality you survey is the*
> *picture it creates.*"

Andy's reply made Janet grin from ear to ear.

"What about our insecurities?" Peter challenged.

Before Andy could reply, I answered Peter's question with a question of my own: "How can you possibly have an insecure thought without a thought?"

Peter slowly moved his head up and down in acknowledgment of my answer.

"You know, Peter," I said, "when I first listened to Andy a year ago, I felt the way you do. And to be honest, I still don't comprehend very much of what he is trying to tell us. But more and more each day, I'm starting to understand that I can change my own thoughts to a more positive outlook on life—and that such a change will be enormously beneficial to me."

"It really shows," Peter said. "You look great. You must be doing something right to be so successful and so happy at the same time! I'd certainly like to know what it is."

With great bitterness, Tom declared that Andy's answers were simply outside the scope of psychology and that he completely failed to see the relationship between what Andy was saying and the study of mental health.

All four of us looked over at the gardener, wondering what he would say to this.

As usual, he didn't answer the way we expected he would. In his very quiet English voice, Andy said, "Let's journey down another path and have a closer look at what my simple mind is trying to convey. Please be patient with me. After all, I don't have an advanced education like you learned doctors; I only have a degree in agriculture and I'm sure our vocabularies will differ considerably. These three gifts I just talked about are the filters of your *soul*. Or, as you psychologists would probably prefer to say, these three gifts are the filters to your *psyche*. When any one of these filters gets obscured, we fail to see life with any degree of clarity. This in turn leads to what I believe you therapists sometimes call a dysfunctional life."Then with an immense grin on his face, Andy asked us to excuse him for a little while so he could gather some tools for his next task.

Chapter 5

The Nature of Thought

*A*fter Andy left, Tom had no hesitation in letting us know that he thought the old gardener was as crazy as a hoot owl.

Janet suggested, "Perhaps we shouldn't judge the man. After all, we did ask for his opinion. He's simply putting in his two bits' worth, just like us."

Tom resolutely insisted that the gardener had no right to make such outlandish statements. "Personally, I think it might be a good idea if your gardener friend sought some professional help, Eric. I think he's more than a little delusional," he fumed.

Janet asked Tom why he was getting so upset by the old gardener's words. "If you think he's delusional, why are you bothered by what he says?" she gently prodded. "Surely you should be above letting him get to you."

Peter listened to Janet, then said, "Wait a minute! Janet's correct in her observation. Why *are* we letting this old guy get to us? I mean, we are all qualified therapists who should be able to entertain the occasional new theory without becoming upset, regardless of its source."

Tom stubbornly resisted. "There is nothing to think about," he sputtered. "As far as I'm concerned, the old gardener was talking nonsense. *That* is what's bothering me."

I started to tell Tom about my trip to India— that I had met enlightened people who talked in a mystical manner, and how at times they had my mind totally confused. But instead I surprised even myself by saying, "Who knows? Maybe Andy is enlightened."

"That's a laugh," said Tom. "An enlightened gardener!"

"I know the possibility is remote," I conceded. "But if Andy *is* enlightened, do you have any idea how lucky we are to be here talking with him? After all, some people travel all over the world searching for such a person and never find one."

No sooner had I said these words then Andy returned with his tools. "I really have to do some work or I'll be getting sacked from my job," he said with a bright smile.

I asked Andy if he would answer just one more question before we left him to his work. He nodded his agreement.

"What difference do you see between the things you talk about and some of the present, widely accepted theories of psychology?" I asked.

The gardener answered, "I don't rightly know

what you people believe or don't believe. I only know what I know: Within the soul of all human beings, there lies an innate spiritual knowledge that has the power to repair mental disturbances."

Turning his gaze to me, Andy said, "Eric, do you remember how I told you last year that *Thought* is spiritually based, and that if you could understand my words, you would have success beyond anything you had ever witnessed?"

Startled by his question, I asked, "Just like Mrs. Taylor?"

"Yes, just like Mrs. Taylor and the others who say their lives have changed because they heard something regarding their thoughts—not through analyzing their thoughts, but by seeing the *power of Thought* itself."

All four of us sat bemused by Andy's reply, not knowing what to say. Finally I asked Andy, "Are you trying to tell us that some of my clients are finding their own innate wisdom?"

"Can you give me a better explanation for what has been happening?" he replied.

Both Tom and Peter immediately disagreed, saying it was their fervent belief that wisdom had to be taught, and that time and patience also had a lot to do with finding wisdom.

"That's an old wives' tale—a sheer fallacy," Andy said dismissively. "Wisdom is not connected to age; wisdom is an innate spiritual intelligence that lies within the soul of every human being on earth, hidden only by our contaminated thoughts. This is why one must look *within* for true knowledge."

Andy became very serious then, asking us to listen carefully to what he was about to say and to try listening with an open mind to discover something lying beyond the beliefs we now possessed. "After all," he said softly, "you have to remember that you are looking for the *unknown*, not the known. May I therefore suggest that you listen not with these two external ears that stick out of your head, but with an inner ear that lies deep within your soul."

Speaking directly to me, Andy said, "When you told Mrs. Taylor that it was her *own* thinking that had been creating many of her miserable feelings about life, your words opened her mind to another level of understanding, which for a moment in time took her back to *Original Thought*. Let's say your words triggered something inside her consciousness that took her back to when her mind was purer, *before* her nightmarish behavior patterns started, thus giving her a new start in life. One could say her mind was elevated to a new level, and once the mind has been elevated, it will never return permanently to its original state."

"Astonishing! How could one simple observation or insight have such a profound impact on someone?" Peter marveled.

Andy's piercing blue eyes locked with Peter's, then he said, "Never underestimate the power of an *insight*, young man. Sometimes one genuine insight is worth all your previous experiences in life put together."

Turning back to me, Andy continued, "May I suggest to you that Mrs. Taylor had more than just an inkling. Clearly, she attained a fairly deep understanding that her debilitating memories were being kept alive by her own continuous digging through the rubble of her past, that her own thoughts were holding her a prisoner of her yesterdays and making her present existence unbearable. The way I see it, your Mrs. Taylor realized that she had been blaming her past circumstances for her present-day state. She suddenly recognized that she was herself the sole author of her present condition."

I was amazed by how astutely Andy explained Mrs. Taylor's recovery, and by how correctly he described how she had admitted that her own malformed thoughts and negative feelings played a big role in her desperately unhappy life. As I sat there listening to Andy, there was no doubt in my mind that all of my recent clients had responded in a beautiful way to the realization that their thinking was directly linked to some of their problems.

It was after just such an office experience that my partner and I realized to a deeper extent that we had stumbled upon something different, something that was beyond our training. We could see that some real healing was somehow happening in our patients, even though we explained very little to them about the thought process. Furthermore, we were consistently amazed by what the patients would say to us when describing their new understanding of themselves. That is why I wanted to further investigate Andy's unusual theory that *Thought* was the missing link that we therapists had been searching for. So I asked the gardener to explain his theory of *Thought* again.

Pointing to a nearby shrub, Andy said, "Take that rose bush, for example. We are all looking at the same plant, but our perception of it varies according to the way we each think and see. One person may see a vigorous rose, another may see a rose that could benefit from a little pruning, and a third might see a mess that no amount of attention would save. The rose bush isn't changing; it's the way we personally perceive it that differs, the way each of us thinks that colors our perception."

"It's the same with life," he continued. "It's only natural that a happy person will see life quite differently than an unhappy person will. Again, the secret lies in the perception fashioned from our personal thoughts. Now please remember, I am not judging anyone; I don't care how people use their thoughts. I am not talking in personal terms but in impersonal ones. In complete neutrality, it is my belief that our personal realities are created by using the *power of Thought*."

"What do you mean?" Peter questioned. "Are

you suggesting that we actually create the reality that is all around us in our own minds?"

Andy stroked his chin as he contemplated the best answer to Peter's question. "What I mean is, our manner of coping with life evolves from our personal thoughts and the way these thoughts cause us to relate to each new day. Never forget, your thoughts and feelings are the blueprints from which your personal reality is built. Change your blueprints and the reality changes accordingly. My advice is to use your thoughts and feelings wisely, and they will never let you down.

"As therapists you should understand that *Thought* is the vehicle that will take you to the secret knowledge that lies at the root of all human experience here on earth. And you should always remember,

Thought is not written in stone.
It is fluid and can be molded to suit
the day.

Universal Thought is the creative agent we use to direct ourselves through this spiritual experience called life."

There was dead silence for the longest time as we tried to fathom the meaning of the gardener's unusual words. Andy picked up his shovel and dug into the soft, rich soil. As he positioned a small plant, he turned to Peter. "What you seek is like a cosmic jigsaw puzzle and, with fate on your side, you may find where some of the pieces fit. From then on, the search for the other missing pieces becomes a wonderful adventure."

Tom snorted and looked away, absently tossing pebbles into the fountain.

"That's an interesting way to put it," Peter admitted.

Andy bowed his head at Peter's acceptance of his words. Then he said, "By the way, Peter, one important piece of this cosmic jigsaw is to realize the fact that intellectual thought is merely a byproduct of *Universal Thought*."

Janet explained to Andy that, as therapists, none of us had ever been taught about the power of thought, let alone a concept like *Universal Thought*.

Peter then eagerly explained to Andy that cognitive therapy deals in positive thought and doesn't go back into the past as many other approaches do. "However, its practitioners *do* concentrate on the contents of our thoughts, and as far as I know they don't put as much emphasis on the role of mind or thought as you seem to do."

Andy sat in silence as he listened to Peter's brief explanation of the correlation between thought and cognitive therapy.

"Is there any difference between what you were talking about and cognitive therapy, Andy?" Janet asked.

"I really don't have any idea what cognitive therapists believe or don't believe," he answered. "I'm no therapist, Luv. I only know what I know, and what I am saying doesn't only apply to you four because you are therapists. What I am saying pertains to every human being in the world."

Tom continued to look away and remained aloof from the conversation, but I had a strong feeling that he was listening more closely than he cared to let on. I asked Andy to talk more about the difference between our personal thoughts and what he was calling the divine gift of *Universal Thought*.

The gardener's reply excited me. "The way I see it, Eric, *Universal Thought*, accompanied by our free will, gives us the ability to experience life. But remember, my friend, how you use this gift is entirely up to you."

Janet also appeared excited. "So what I hear you saying is, How we use our thoughts is up to us, whether we use them wisely or foolishly."

"Yes, Luv, that is exactly what I am saying."

"But Andy," Janet continued, "I can't imagine how many different thoughts everyone in the world has each and every day."

"An infinite number," Andy replied. "But remember those are *personal* thoughts that can be broken down into an infinite number of segments. However, the source called *Universal Thought* is spiritual by nature and completely neutral, just like *Mind* and *Consciousness*. All three sources are elemental and cannot be split into particles; they are the three constants that envelop all creatures great and small and allow us to experience life."

Then Tom finally joined the conversation by

muttering that if he told some of his associates that psychology could be explained with three universal principles, they would ridicule him.

With his foot on the shovel, Andy casually responded, "Then I can guarantee you that your associates will never find the answers they seek."

The assurance in Andy's voice shocked the four of us into complete silence for the longest time.

Finally, Peter's inquisitive mind rebounded and he eagerly asked Andy, "What is the difference between what you are calling *Universal Thought* and intellectual thought?"

"None," the gardener replied. "They are both the *same power* being used differently."

Tom looked extremely disturbed by Andy's statements and asked him to define *Mind*.

The gardener dropped his head as if in deep thought, then said, "*Mind*, when accompanied by *Thought* and *Consciousness*, is the master weaver that creates the fabric of cause and effect."

"I don't want to appear rude," Tom interjected, "but you're making no sense at all. And besides, the things you're saying have more to do with philosophy or religion than psychology."

Andy smiled. "I am not talking religion, Tom. Perhaps I am talking spiritual truth, but I can assure you that the answer you seek *is* spiritual. The basis of psychology stems from spiritual truth. If you were to investigate the words of many wise philosophers, you would find they all agree on one thing: Simplicity holds the answer to acquiring mystical knowledge. In simplicity lies complexity, and complexity can be reduced to simplicity."

Tom sat dumbstruck by Andy's paradoxical reply. Clearly captivated, Janet's eyes danced from one speaker to another, her quick mind absorbing every word that was being said. I could feel Peter's confusion and Janet's fascination with the entire conversation. Then Janet asked, "Why do you refer to *mystical* knowledge?"

"Because mystics see beyond the contamination of their intellectual minds," Andy replied.

"I don't quite get it," Janet admitted. "Could you try phrasing it a different way?"

The old gardener scratched his forehead. "Well, Luv, you could say they talk directly from an inner knowledge that can only be explained metaphorically."

"This is heavy-duty stuff," said Peter. "I think I must be missing something. Can you tell me why these so-called mystics aren't just more direct in what they're trying to relate?"

"They probably are, in their own special way," Andy replied. "But sometimes the true meaning, the meaning beyond the words, can quite easily get lost in the transmission between speaker and listener."

Before anyone could ask another question, the gardener tipped his cap and—explaining that it was time for him to have lunch—left us to ponder over his latest statements.

Chapter 6

Original Thought

*A*fter Andy left, we made our way back to the hotel to have our own lunch. Tom, again being his usual argumentative self, brought up the amazing recovery of Mrs. Taylor. "In actual fact, Mrs. Taylor is just going into denial, is she not?" he demanded.

"Maybe old Andy just has an overactive imagination," Peter remarked with a shrug. "After all, how could he possibly know all that he claimed to know about Mrs. Taylor and her father?"

"That is the fascinating thing, Peter," I interjected. "He was dead on with his observations regarding Mrs. Taylor and her father, and I have a strong suspicion that it was not just a good guess on his part."

I explained to Tom that I too had initially suspected that Mrs. Taylor was going into denial. But the more I listened to her, the more convinced I became that the woman had undergone a unique experience beyond anything I had ever witnessed before. In my professional opinion, she definitely wasn't in denial. "I tell you, Tom, it astonished me to hear how she talked about her past in an entirely different, more positive and rational way than she had when she first came to my office. It was as if she had gone through some kind of metamorphosis."

"What was her diagnosis?" Peter asked.

"She suffered from clinical depression," I replied. "Her father was an alcoholic who was both physically and verbally abusive, and her painful and unpleasant memories made it very difficult for her to forgive him. For years, she carried this heavy load of old, unforgiving, negative feelings towards her father. They had made her a very bitter person. Now this same Mrs. Taylor says she can see the innocence in her father's behavior and feels sorry for him. She talks about how much he must have been suffering to have acted the way he did and to have found relief only when he was drunk."

"That's quite a story," Peter said. "That's true forgiveness if I ever heard it. What is the nature of their relationship now?"

"They see each other more now than they ever did before, and apparently they are beginning to become the best of friends. Something I didn't tell you was that Mrs. Taylor's father had stopped drinking approximately three months prior to her visit to my office. When she told her father what had happened during our session together, unbelievable as it sounds, her father clued in to this theory of thought almost immediately. And, to the amazement of his daughter, he announced that he realized that by constantly thinking about his own condition he had only unwittingly kept it alive. He came to realize that some of the therapy he was undergoing for his alcoholism was just aggravating his situation by keeping old negative feelings alive. He explained to his daughter that his therapy group was mostly confrontational, that it was constantly urging him to talk about his problems. He admitted to her that he regularly felt awful after attending the sessions, even remarking that he often wished they could be more lighthearted.

"After hearing Mrs. Taylor talk about her father, I sat dumbfounded, completely unable to respond to her. Neither my partner nor I had ever been taught that a person's thoughts had anything to do with their drinking habits—or any other habit or addiction for that matter."

At this point Peter commented, "I can see how a patient would be a mentally healthy person *before* going through a traumatic experience. That makes sense. But I just can't follow Andy's logic regarding *original* thought."

Tom huffily asserted that he was taught that there was no such thing as *original* thought—that anything being taught today was, of necessity, built on yesterday's knowledge. "Or, as someone once said to me," he expounded, "'Today's knowledge is a descendent of yesterday's.'"

"At school I was taught much the same as Tom," Peter said. "I was told that there was no such thing as original thought. I'd sure like to ask your gardener friend a few more questions about his views on this."

"Now's your chance," I said, glancing out the window. "There he is, working on the lawn."

After finishing our lunch, we made our way to where Andy was working. Before long, Tom and Peter were bombarding him with questions while Janet looked on in fascination. Listening to my colleagues debate original thought with the gardener, I felt they would soon overwhelm poor Andy with their multitude of questions—and I wondered how he could possibly answer them all.

Andy bowed his head as if he were in deep contemplation, took a handkerchief out of his back pocket, blew his nose, and then, with a waggish smile, addressed Tom and Peter.

"All I can tell you gentlemen is the way I see life. The way it appears to me, original thought lies deep within the soul of all human beings and is revealed by a true *realization*—or if you wish, an *insight* beyond the intellect."

Without giving himself time to absorb Andy's answer, Peter immediately asked the gardener why he had separated the intellect and wisdom.

Suddenly looking quite stern, the gardener suggested that Peter should learn to listen to what he was told before asking more questions.

"I don't know how you psychologists see things," Andy continued, "but the way I see it, there are two types of knowledge. One type is our *intellectual* knowledge, which is connected to our learned and memorized understanding and experience of life. The second knowledge I speak of is *spiritual* in nature and lies deep within the soul of all human beings."

Now I simply had to join the conversation. "Are you trying to tell us that you believe there's a spiritual knowledge that is present in the soul of all human beings—before *any* human experience?" I asked.

Andy paused to reflect before replying, "Yes. Sometimes people call this spiritual knowledge *wisdom*. The way I see it, your Mrs. Taylor found some purer thoughts from deep within her own consciousness."

With a smile, the gardener turned, looked straight at Tom and said, "I believe Mrs. Taylor found some original thought. And what she found was something she could never explain, because what she found was beyond the word."

Andy's voice softened, "As I told you before, Eric, the belief that it takes time to find wisdom is one of the greatest fallacies on earth. Wisdom is not learned—it is unfolded from within one's own consciousness.

"When such knowledge appears to a person, it is revealed in a form that some may call an insight. Others may call it a revelation. No matter what you call it, for a fleeting moment in time, your Mrs. Taylor stopped her chattering *personal mind* long enough to find some of her own inner wisdom."

"That's a very interesting way of explaining Mrs. Taylor's recovery," I said. "I had never even considered the idea that Mrs. Taylor found her *own* wisdom. I always thought it must have been related to something I had said to her, some words from *my* understanding of her situation. Surely I get some praise for Mrs. Taylor's recovery?"

Smiling at my plaintive tone, Andy said, "Of course you do. You should be proud of your success. After all, Eric, you are the one who helped her find her peace of mind."

Tom responded sarcastically, "So all Eric has to do is repeat the same magic words to his next client and he'll get the same miraculous results?"

With a very serious look on his face the old gardener replied, "Tom, what you have to realize is this: It is not the words but what is *beyond* the words that is important. It has been my experience in life that no matter how strong or how clever a teacher you may be, if someone is unwilling to change and refuses to listen, there is nothing you or anyone else can do to help improve his or her condition. You know the old saying, 'You can lead a horse to water, but you can't make it drink.'"

"So, what about those who are so far gone we therapists can't reach them?" asked Janet.

"I suggest you do what you normally do," Andy replied. "Give them lots of love and care—

but be sure you don't assume too readily that anyone is beyond help."

I asked Andy to explain what he had said to Tom in another way. As he began his explanation, I initially thought he hadn't heard my question properly when he said, "Eric, you told me that when you were in India you spent a considerable amount of time meditating, yet you were not successful in finding the elusive wisdom you sought."

"No, I wasn't successful," I admitted, "and that's what I can't understand. Why would people who were not even meditating find wisdom?"

Smiling, Andy replied, "Correct me if I'm wrong, but I have the suspicion that perhaps you are a little confused about the difference between the *act* of meditating and the *state* of meditation. Just because you're not in the accepted physical posture or chanting a mantra doesn't mean a thing. I have friends who find that tranquil state of meditation when they fish. Others find peace of mind while taking a walk, working in the garden or playing golf. For many others, it is a structured ritual requiring great dedication. There are a great many different ways to reach such a state."

Janet mused, "It's strange you should explain meditation that way. When I was a young girl, my favorite place to find serenity was sitting on a rocking chair under the old weeping willow in our back yard. As a teenager, I would spend countless hours contemplating anything and everything, and many times I found the peaceful state of mind you just spoke of. But, I never considered that I was meditating."

As Janet finished speaking, Andy stood up and thanked us for an interesting conversation. Then he excused himself, saying he had work to do and that he was a little bit behind with his chores.

Chapter 7

Freedom from the Past

*A*fter the gardener left, the four of us looked at each other in total disbelief and burst into peals of laughter.

"You were right," Peter said. "The old guy is rather enigmatic, to say the least. But like Tom, I can't help but think that maybe he just has the gift of the blarney. I seriously doubt that many of his assumptions will hold water. Personally, I think he's just a nice old man who loves to talk."

"I can't imagine how he came up with all his unusual notions," Janet added. "I have to admit, he certainly is a unique character. You definitely don't meet someone like him every day—at least I don't! But whether or not there's any validity to what he is saying is another matter. And yet, I instinctively feel that there is truth in some of what he says. I'd sure like to talk with him again, if for no other reason than sheer curiosity."

That evening at supper, the entire restaurant was abuzz with people discussing the presentations of the day's speakers. Our table was no different, except that we talked about the gardener.

We discussed our feelings and our thoughts about Andy's unusual theories on life. Janet and I agreed that his philosophical views were powerful and had the ring of truth to them. Tom and Peter, on the other hand, were definitely skeptical of everything the gardener had said. Tom had a particularly hard time giving any credibility to the gardener's views.

I attempted to explain to Tom and Peter that it had become clearer and clearer to me during the past year just how much my thoughts controlled my own personal life.

Peter became very serious. "Eric, it's very obvious that you are seeing something I'm not. Correct me if I'm wrong, but what I am hearing you say is that you are starting to believe that thoughts are one of the main sources of everyone's behavior and that thoughts are also the basis of all our personal realities."

"When you think about it Peter, how could we possibly function as human beings without thought?" I asked.

"That may be true," Peter responded. "Maybe we couldn't function without thoughts. But what good will that knowledge do me?"

Janet interrupted before I could answer Peter's question. "You know, all my life, as far as I can remember, I've always wondered to what extent our thoughts affected our lives," she said.

"That's why I've always figured it is cruel to take clients back into past traumatic experiences and watch them needlessly reliving their hellish ordeals. When you think about it, all we are doing is asking them to keep dwelling on things that are painful to them. As a therapist, I've honestly never seen it do much good. This new approach of yours, Eric, sounds much gentler and friendlier—and if it works, it would be incredible."

"Do you think that some of your clients honestly believe they are actually starting to free themselves from their traumatic experiences and memories of their childhood?" Tom demanded skeptically. "We all know that our personal and mental structure is learned at an early age and can't be changed. As far as I'm concerned, the most you can teach people is how to cope."

"You know, Tom, I once asked Andy about that very thing," I replied. "Do you know what he said? 'Merely coping with your memories is like putting a bucket under a leaky roof. It would be only a temporary solution and, in the long run, of very little value. It might even allow the original problem to get worse.'"

Janet suggested to Tom that his negative outlook in life wouldn't give himself or his clients much hope. "What was it Andy said today?" she mused. "Oh yes, he said,

*'All you have to do is realize
that the past is now only a
ghostly memory
kept alive by digging into the
archives of your own stagnated
memories.'"*

Tears began to run down Janet's cheeks as she said, "I have to admit these are very powerful words. I don't know why, but they mean a lot to me. I feel them right here," she said, pointing to her heart.

This was the first time I'd ever seen this kind of reaction from Janet, and I'd certainly never before heard such interesting and profound philosophical discussions between Janet, Tom and Peter. Whatever the gardener was saying, he was certainly having quite an effect on the four of us.

Peter said, "I just remembered a professor in college, Professor Allan, who told me that all the research he had done on mental health indicated that it was always the patients' thoughts which dictated the final course of their actions. I don't think he felt people could control the contents of their thoughts. But he had a strong suspicion that thoughts are somehow connected to an inevitable outcome. That professor didn't have the answer to how it all worked, but he was certainly trying his best. He was a really nice guy and a damn good teacher." Then, with a chuckle, he said, "I wonder what Professor Allan would think of this conversation?"

Chapter 8
Thought and Change

$\mathcal{B}$oth Peter and Tom continued to be disturbed by some of the gardener's statements. After reflecting on some of his philosophical views, they decided that they wanted to challenge him. So the following day, after our scheduled meeting, we decided to gather once again at the fountain where Andy had been working. When we arrived, there was no sign of the gardener, but we were sure he couldn't be far off. We spent a blissful few minutes lounging on the lawn, enjoying the summer weather.

"I can't believe it," Peter said. "Here we are, four qualified practitioners at a serious, professional convention, asking some old gardener for information that might assist us in our practice. Do you have the feeling there is something amiss?"

With a large grin on her face, Janet said, "Why not seek information where we find it? Who knows? Maybe the old guy does have something worthwhile to say. I know one thing—whatever he said yesterday sure got to me. After all, even though Freud was a highly educated man, he had absolutely no psychological training. He created his theories from his own personal observations of life with the best scientific methodology available at the time."

"That's true," I said. "Freud had no more training in the psychological field than Andy does. What if, by mere chance, Andy does know something that we don't?"

"And maybe pigs can fly!" Tom snapped.

Janet completely ignored Tom's sarcastic remark, saying, "When you think of it, many major discoveries throughout history were initially refuted, even deliberately suppressed by various professions and universities. For example, when Dr. Lister suggested that germs were the cause of infection, recommending that surgeons should scrub up before an operation and that surgical instruments should be sterilized, he was ridiculed and scorned by his colleagues in the Royal College of Surgeons."

"Even obvious solutions to pressing problems," I added, "are sometimes buried by the prevailing views. I learned recently that it took more than 100 years of persistence for a simple clockmaker's solution to the problem of determining longitude to gain acceptance. The astronomers in those days were so sure that the answer was complex and difficult that they scoffed at an uneducated clockmaker's simple answer to their difficulty. According to history, they continued to delay trials and impose special conditions on the clockmaker's idea for years, even though ships and lives were being lost regularly because of the lack of a reliable means of calculating longitude."

"Yes," Janet agreed. "I recall that story. The astronomers thought the clockmaker was just too ignorant about navigational calculations. They constantly blocked efforts to test his specially designed clocks aboard ships because he was not an astronomer and therefore, in their view, couldn't begin to understand the problem. They couldn't see that something as simple as keeping accurate time aboard ships could have anything to do with something so difficult as reckoning their location on the high seas."

"And yet," I said, "it seems incredible to us now— absolutely ludicrous—that they would not even take the time for an honest look at the solution the clockmaker was suggesting."

"Their egos probably got in the way and they didn't want the world to know that a clockmaker discovered the solution to a navigator's problem," Peter responded. "I imagine some people would find such a situation embarrassing."

Janet shot Peter a meaningful look. "I think one of the failures of many people is to reject that which they know little about!"

At that moment, a pretty young woman approached us and introduced herself as Helen, the assistant manager of the hotel. She graciously asked if everything was going well with our conference and if our accommodations were to our satisfaction. We assured her that everything was more than we had expected and thanked her for her concern, commenting on the attractiveness of the hotel and the grounds.

"Wonderful!" she responded. "And please, if you want anything, just let us know and we will do our best to accommodate you."

On a whim, I asked Helen if she had seen the gardener today.

"You mean Andy? Yes, I saw him heading towards the garden shed. Is anything wrong?"

"No, no," I assured her. "We just wanted to have a little talk with him. Have you known Andy very long?"

"I've known Andy approximately five years now," she said with a smile, "and I can honestly say he is a good friend who helped save my life."

"What do you mean, he helped save your life?" I asked. The manager hesitated for a few moments, so I quickly softened my tone, hoping to put her at ease. "We really are amazed by much of what Andy has to say—and we'd love to hear your story."

Smiling, the manager began to speak. "I first started working here as a dishwasher in the kitchen, and at that time my life was in a total shambles. I was an alcoholic, barely coping with everyday living. I was seeing a therapist for my problem and I also belonged to an alcoholics' organization, but things still weren't looking too rosy. One day, roughly four and a half years ago, I was in such rough shape that I found myself crying and gasping for a breath of fresh air as I was scrubbing pots, so I went outside and sat on the lawn. I was feeling very sorry for myself, and wondered just how bad my life could get. I had lost all hope.

"Just when I was at my lowest state of mind, Andy came along. Seeing that I was crying, he came over to comfort me. We talked about all sorts of things and I remember we started to laugh at something. I forget what it was. Then, for no apparent reason, it was as if a huge dam burst in my head and I started to cry with tears of joy. Since that day I haven't had one single drink." It was obvious that Helen was affected by her own story; her voiced faltered and she fought back tears. "What's more, I have had no desire to drink."

Totally under control again, she said, "I always look forward to having little chats with Andy. Do you know he's been in many parts of the world? He has lots of very interesting stories about his adventures and travels."

Peter obviously found her story intriguing. "I wonder if you would mind answering a few questions?" he asked. "For example, what did you and Andy talk about?"

With a conspiratorial smile that included us all, she answered, "You've all heard Andy talk, haven't you? Half the time you have no idea what he's saying. I can't begin to remember what we talked about. All I know is that for the following fortnight after we spoke I never touched a drop of liquor. What was even more unusual, I didn't even realize during that entire two week period that I wasn't drinking. I just didn't *think* about it, at all! To me it was miraculous."

"Surely you must remember some of your conversation," Peter prodded.

"I do remember we talked about *Thought* quite a lot. But the thing that stands out most vividly in my memory was the *feeling*. I can't explain it. As I said, it was more of a wonderful *feeling* than an understanding of his words. Andy is quite spiritual. In fact you might say he is rather a free spirit," she quipped. "He most certainly has his own ways, but he's a likable person and has definitely been a good friend to me."

No one said anything for the longest time. Finally, Tom broke the silence by asking in a dubious tone, "Are you trying to tell us that you just suddenly stopped drinking? Just like that?" He snapped his fingers for emphasis.

"Yes," Helen replied. "As soon as I saw I was responsible for my own thoughts, and that it was my own thoughts that were creating my emotional state, that was it!"

The four of us stared at the young lady, then at each other, in total disbelief. We found it difficult to accept what we were hearing, this further evidence of the connection between thoughts and behavior. Then Janet inquired, "Surely it couldn't be that simple. What did you do to help you stop drinking?"

"Nothing. It just happened. It seemed miraculous. As I said, once I understood the power of my own thinking on a deeper level it just happened; there was nothing to do. I remember one thing Andy said. He told me, if I could, to learn to

> *'Do without doing and think*
> *without thinking.'*"

"That's utter nonsense," Tom exploded. "Sheer gobbledy-gook!"

Peter half-heartedly agreed. "How can you do and think without doing and thinking?"

Nodding her head, the manager replied, "I asked Andy that very same question, and he told me it was something I had to figure out for myself. But he did say it had something to do with *faith* and a *silent mind*. He also said the secret we all seek lies in the state of '*no thought*.'"

Janet said she had never in her life had so many goosebumps and shudders.

"Do you still go to your alcohol prevention meetings?" I asked.

Smiling, the manager said, "Oh, no! I really have no need for them any more."

I asked her about her therapist's reaction to what had happened.

"He wasn't too impressed," Helen admitted.

"How did he feel about your not attending any more meetings?"

"He felt I should continue with my treatment and my support group meetings. I was actually very surprised by his reaction. He became rather upset when I tried to explain that I had realized that it was my own thoughts that had been creating a good many of my problems. He just couldn't hear what I was saying. The interesting thing is, he still has the same problem I had four and a half years ago!"

As the four of us stood dumbfounded by the story the young lady had just told, she treated us to her beautiful smile and, in a cheery voice, wished us good day and left.

"That's quite the story," Janet declared.

A few minutes later, Andy arrived with a bag of lime in his old, battered wheelbarrow. After explaining to us that the soil around the fountain was sour, he said,

"Just like love and wisdom sweeten
the soul, lime sweetens the soil."

We told Andy that we had been talking to the assistant manager and thought she was a very interesting lady.

"As a matter of fact," I said, "we were just remarking on how the entire staff at this hotel is the happiest and most helpful we have ever encountered."

Andy agreed. "Yes, they are a nice bunch of people. And isn't it wonderful that a woman as young as Helen can keep this place running like clockwork? She really is a great asset to the hotel."

Chapter 9

Forgiveness

As Andy lifted the bag of lime from the wheelbarrow and opened it, we sat down near the fountain to continue our conversation.

I asked Andy why he once made the statement that going back into the past to fix today's problems was like psychological suicide.

Wiping his hands on his pants legs, he said, "I realize I'm not educated like you doctors, but common sense tells me those past experiences no longer actually exist. Only in memory do they remain alive. Only in here," he said, pointing to his head.

Tom objected, "Surely our past traumatic experiences were real?"

"Yes, Tom they were a reality when they happened. But now they only exist in our minds, as memories; they are only pictures embedded in our consciousness. My advice, Tom, is:

Tread not into yesterday's sorrows,
For they are the pathways
of despair."

"Try to be more charitable and open to change," Andy continued. "Allow yourself to live without yesterday's burdens on your mind and it will make today a more pleasant experience. I realize that, at times, past experiences may appear as realistic *representations*, but they are not real *now*. They are merely memories. Don't you see that holding on to such harmful *memories* and *feelings*—and constantly retrieving them from the archives of your mind so that you can revisit them—holds you a prisoner of your now-departed past?

> *Let the past be dead and let the*
> *dead rest in peace.*"

There was a prolonged silence after these words. Then Tom, obviously looking for an argument, suddenly turned to Andy and said, "You're asking people to go into denial."

"No, not at all," Andy replied calmly. "What I am suggesting is forgiveness."

Tom was startled. "Forgiveness? What has forgiveness got to do with this?"

Andy rested his chin on his shovel handle and stood quietly, as he often did while thinking. After a few moments of reflection, he answered. "As far as I'm concerned, negative memories and feelings are like scratches on your spectacles. They obscure your vision. Naturally, if your spectacles are full of scratches, it can be very difficult to see through them. Your vision becomes impaired, preventing you from seeing life with any clarity. I assure you, one of the most effective scratch removers for the human mind is *forgiveness*. Remember Tom,

> *Our eyes are the windows*
> *to the soul,*
> *And only when our eyes are free of*
> *yesterday's scratches*
> *Will we see today with any clarity."*

Janet asked, "So what you are saying is that people have to realize that their memories are only phantoms, kept alive by their own *thoughts*?"

"That is exactly what I am saying."

"Easier said than done," said Tom, obviously disturbed by the gardener's views.

Andy shoveled some lime into a spreader, wiped his hands with an old cloth which hung from his back pocket, looked down at the ground for the longest time, then spoke. "My friend, what you have to realize is that life is too short to travel back into the black clouds of yesterday. My advice is to forget all theories that take you back into the past. You have to try to realize that happiness and contentment come when the human mind breaks the chains of yesterday's bondage. The laws are simple:

*Forget the problems of yesterday,
learn to count today's blessings
and you will be well rewarded."*

Smiling, Andy continued, "The human mind is like a garden, and when one plants even the best of seeds in poor soil the crop will be poor. Conversely, when the poorest of men plants virtuous thoughts, he may indeed become a king in his own world."

Directly addressing Tom, Andy explained, "Every one of us has a mental waste basket and we would all be a lot healthier if we learned to use it."

Again, Tom appeared somewhat agitated by Andy's words and replied, "If it were that easy, don't you think that Freud and all the other giants of psychology would have known about it? I think this whole discussion is an insult to the memory of Freud."

Andy pulled no punches, replying, "Sir, believe me, there is no way I would dishonor Freud. But think of it this way: If aeronautical engineers had stagnated in outdated thoughts as you have, we would still be flying planes of the same design the Wright brothers invented. I have no doubt that even though we now fly in supersonic jets, modern aeronautical engineers have the highest respect and regard for the Wright brothers' pioneering work in their field."

"Let me get this straight," said Peter. "Are you saying our personal thoughts have a great bearing on how we experience life, and that past events don't necessarily have to determine our present condition?"

"Yes, that is exactly what I am saying," Andy answered. "However, the main thing you have to realize is this: The answer you seek lies not in our *separate* beliefs, but in the realization that *Thought* is one of the common denominators in *all* psychological and spiritual understanding. Now please remember that I'm not talking about the personal psychology that you practice. That is your business. What I'm saying touches everyone in this world—whether he be beggar or king, rich or poor, important or unknown. It doesn't matter who one is; we are all guided through life by our own thought systems. How we relate to life as a whole is conditioned by our thinking. I'm talking about a *logic of the psyche—before form.*"

"What do you mean by 'logic of the psyche before form?'" I asked.

"That I cannot explain," the gardener replied. "All I can tell you is, such knowledge is completely impersonal and therefore completely neutral. As I said, it is before form."

Janet commented, "That's a fascinating premise, and sitting here listening to you, I am just starting to understand to a deeper degree the implications of *Thought* in our lives. This is truly amazing!"

Again, Tom defiantly announced that the way the gardener was talking was far too simplistic.

"Your theories won't hold water," he railed, "because nobody—nobody!—can change their past experiences."

Janet tried to calm Tom by saying, "That's not the way I heard it, Tom. Andy wasn't saying you can *change* your past experiences. What I understood him to say was that you can improve the way you relate to life, if you can stop the useless, negative, historical thoughts and memories from controlling how you comprehend life *now*. Or, as Andy put it, 'without yesterday's scratches on your spectacles.'"

"I still say he is asking us to go into denial," Tom muttered petulantly.

Janet bristled. "Tom, you make me so angry with your endlessly pessimistic way of observing things. Why don't you try to see beyond all your negative thinking and just for once in your life see things in a more positive light?"

Peter intervened, "Hold on, you two, let's not get carried away. After all, we *are* professional counselors. Surely we can discuss this in a rational way and accept our differences."

Andy, who had been sitting back with a bemused expression while we argued with each other, apologized for any bad feelings he may have created among us, then bid us good day and began rolling the lime spreader up and down the lawn.

Lying in bed that evening, I thought back on what an inspiring day it had been. I had enjoyed every minute of it. Closing my eyes, I thought to myself, "I have a funny feeling that I'm going to remember this conference for the rest of my life."

Chapter 10

Thought and Reality

The next morning over breakfast, we talked about Andy and how he appeared to be a man of mystery; he certainly didn't behave or talk like his fellow workers. What was it that was so different about him? I suggested to the others that perhaps Andy was one of those "naturals" that appear from time to time.

Tom, being his usual pompous self, chuckled sarcastically. "A natural what?"

"Remember the story of the clock maker, Mr. Astronomer," Janet snapped, her eyes sparkling.

Tom seemed to be about to respond with a cynical reply, then thought better of such a foolish move, knowing Janet's superior skill in verbal jousting.

At this point I asked Peter what he thought about the old gardener's opinion regarding *Thought* and its being so vital.

"To be truthful with you, Eric, I'm intrigued but fail to see the importance of what he is saying,"

Peter said. "I just can't see the value of thought as the old gardener maintains it. What about you Janet?"

"I'm honestly not sure," she replied. "As I've told you before, a friend of mine back in grad school asked the professor to what degree our thoughts affect our behavior. This professor became absolutely furious with my friend, maintaining that our thoughts had only a minuscule influence on our behavior and were therefore barely worth bothering about."

I immediately disagreed with this professor's theory and explained that it was my belief that our thoughts are very important in our lives. "After all," I said, "it is through thought that we create all the laws and rules of our country. I'm pretty sure our thoughts have a lot more to do with our behavior than we now realize."

Peter nodded his head. "I agree with some of what you are saying. Perhaps our thinking does have a considerable amount of input into our social structure, but I still fail to see how it can influence major changes in behavioral patterns. The big question is, how can we, as therapists, help people change to a healthier state of mind?"

Janet beamed. "Oh, is that all you want to know? Have another cup of coffee, Peter, and I'll explain it all to you."

These words brought a hearty laugh from all of us. When it had finally subsided, Janet looked as if she were deep in thought. Then she excitedly said, "Eric, I'm thinking about what you said about thought and our social structures. To elaborate on that premise, even our religions have to be a product of our thinking. As a matter of fact, all institutions of learning have to be a product of humanity's thoughts. Even our own profession has to be a product of personal ideas and beliefs."

"That is absolute rubbish," Tom declared. "Our thoughts are created from and directly linked to our childhood environment *and* the environment we live in now. We certainly don't have much control over that."

"To be truthful with you," I said soothingly, "I was taught just the same as you were. But I have a very strong suspicion that what Andy is saying is beyond what we were taught at university. I still fail to see the deeper application of *Thought* as Andy describes it, but his unique ideas have certainly given me a lot to ponder. I tell you, when Mrs. Taylor transformed in front of my eyes, I asked my associate to see her—and he was just as perplexed by her response as I was. Naturally, at the beginning, both of us dismissed the whole episode as temporary and superficial."

Tom asked me if my partner now uses this "thought theory" in his practice.

"Most definitely, and he gets wonderful results," I replied. "Not only that, his personal life and his marriage have changed dramatically; he's a different man. I've never seen him so happy. He says his family life is better than it's ever been. All

I can say is, the more he realized the connection between *Thought* and his own life, the more understanding he became of others. Remember the old saying, 'Physician, heal thyself'? Well, that's exactly what happened!"

With a puzzled smile on his face, Peter shook his head from side to side. "Come on, Eric—how is that possible?"

Janet jumped into the conversation. "I'm starting to understand why Eric gave up some of the techniques that we have all employed from time to time. My experiences with techniques have been similar to yours, Eric. They seldom appeared to work for any of the groups I led, or for any other group I attended."

Smiling sheepishly, Peter bowed his head. "Janet, listening to your confession about techniques brings back recent memories I'd rather forget."

"Come on, Peter, what are you embarrassed about, and why do you have that inane grin on your face?" Janet teased.

With a visible effort, Peter altered his grin to a look of extreme solemnity, then explained that a couple of years prior he had been working with a group of people, teaching them the importance of being assertive. "I used assertiveness training techniques with one man who wished to ask his boss for a raise. This particular client felt he was too insecure to even raise the subject, so I gave him my four-day assertiveness special. After a few training sessions, he finally found the courage to confront his boss. Armed to the teeth with all his newfound assertiveness training techniques, my patient had no fear in facing his boss and demanding his raise—thanks to yours truly, Dr. Peter Richards."

"Did he get his raise?" asked Janet.

"No, he got fired," Peter murmured.

"Are you serious?" Janet shrieked. "You must be pulling our legs!"

"Surely you're joking?" Tom snorted.

"No, I'm entirely serious," Peter sighed. "The guy got fired. His boss told him there was no place in his organization for the sort of arrogant and aggressive person my client appeared to be."

At this point Janet completely lost control of her laughter and sprayed a mouthful of coffee all over the floor. Even Tom was laughing and pointing his finger at Peter. "That's a good one," he chuckled.

"All I can say is, I did the very best I could," Peter concluded. "I guess it's always easier in hindsight to see what should have been done."

"Or what should *not* have been done!" Janet remarked. "That poor man! What worries me is that a good many of those exercises are making a comeback, simply because we haven't found anything better to replace them. Generally speaking, it has been my experience as a marriage counselor that when love and compassion are missing in a marriage, the relationship is bound to fracture regardless of what techniques may be applied. If people could only get their egos out of the way and start to care for one another instead of fighting over who's wrong and who's right, there would be far better marriages around the world."

"You're far too much of a romantic, Janet," Tom interjected. "You're not looking at reality! A good fight is often quite healthy for a marriage."

Janet completely ignored Tom's sarcastic remark. "I wonder if Andy is married," she mused.

"I believe he did once mention a wife— named Emily, I think," I answered, wondering what was on Janet's mind.

"Oh, I'd love to meet her," Janet said. "I was extremely impressed by Andy's conviction that if people are encouraged to hold on to old grudges and negative memories, there would be little chance of ridding themselves of the negative feelings and emotions they carry. Come to think of it, it sounds like something my parents would say, and they always had plenty of plain, old-fashioned common sense. I bet Andy and his wife do, too. It really struck home for me when Andy said there was far too little forgiveness in many of the psychological concepts that are widely accepted."

"Why do you think he said that?" Peter asked earnestly.

"I think he means that when you spend your mental energy constantly going back into the past to blame someone, then there isn't much room in your head or your heart for forgiveness," she replied.

We all sat thoughtfully for a moment. "You know, Eric," Janet said, "I would love to talk to you in more depth. Your clinic's success fascinates me. I feel envious, and the way you talk, it sounds to me like the atmosphere at your clinic is dramatically different from that at the place where I work. I don't think I can put up with all the bickering that goes on at my office much longer. Every day our staff are at each others' throats. Each day is like going into a war zone."

"It's interesting you should say that, Janet," I replied. "Just last week my associates and I were talking about hiring another therapist. Maybe you should consider working with us."

"Are you kidding?" she exclaimed. "I'd love to. I would start tomorrow!"

"Tell you what—give me a call when you get back and we can get together and discuss it."

"Eric, you have just made my day!" Janet beamed.

Chapter 11

Rediscovering Mind and Soul

It was Friday morning. A particularly well-known therapist, Dr. Turner, who ran a highly successful live-in care facility outside London, was scheduled to talk about positive thinking and its relationship to mental health.

Within minutes of Dr. Turner's beginning his lecture on the benefits of positive thinking, two therapists in the audience loudly disagreed with him. They claimed that quite often negative thinking was just a matter of facing up to reality. Like Tom, these two men insisted such thinking sometimes showed character—a view with which I disagreed completely.

As the meeting continued, so did the same old never-ending arguments. As usual, everyone had their own ideas and concepts of what was right and what was wrong.

At the morning break, my three colleagues and I sat over coffee and discussed the first few speakers, especially Dr. Turner, who was a dynamic and interesting presenter. He had displayed an incredibly optimistic attitude toward life, despite the number of interruptions he endured from the two London practitioners who had continually badgered him during his lecture.

This led us back to our discussions about the old gardener and his unusual ideas. Peter admitted that listening to the old gardener was quite a bit different from sitting through the lectures we had attended. Then he said, "I've been mulling over some of the things Andy said. I'd like to ask him why he put such emphasis on forgiveness."

Janet immediately suggested we all play hooky from the next session, and, if possible, have some more talks with the gardener. Peter and I enthusiastically seconded the motion, while Tom somewhat reluctantly agreed to join us.

The gardens were not extensive but were cunningly designed to give the impression of space and vast variety, so we meandered through them for a bit, admiring the beauty and sticking our noses into some charming nooks and crannies. Finally we came upon Andy at the fish pond, feeding the fish. As usual, he greeted us with his congenial smile and a tip of his hat.

"Good morning, doctors. How is your conference going?"

"Not too badly," Peter replied. "But it's refreshing to take a stroll through the grounds and get a breath of fresh air. As a matter of fact, we were hoping that we might run into you and ask you a few questions regarding the conversation we had the other day."

"Oh! What questions would they be?" Andy said with a twinkle in his eye.

Without delay, Peter asked the gardener about his earlier statement that forgiveness led to peace of mind. "Why do you believe this to be so?"

The old gardener continued feeding the fish, leaving us in suspense. He stroked his chin for a short while, then said, "Surely it is only common sense. When emotions such as vengeance, resentment or lack of forgiveness exist in our hearts, we start to live in a world of negative feelings such as jealousy, hate, envy and selfishness. When a person is in this state, many ill thoughts torment the soul."

"Believe me," he continued, "you will never help anybody by encouraging them to get into their *feelings* of anger or hate. The way I see it, *feelings* are thoughts in action. What you have to realize is that *feelings* are a barometer of the soul and if your heart and mind are full of anger and *negative feelings*, it is a sure sign that life is going to be stormy."

"On the other hand," he concluded, "if you host *positive feelings*, it's a sure sign that life will be calmer and sunnier. Let's just say,

> *Love is the passageway to heaven*
> *and hate is the passageway to hell*."

"But, what if a person has a reasonable right to be angry?" Peter insisted.

"Peter, I'm not judging one's right to be angry or not to be angry," Andy said. "I'm speaking about the *impersonal,* not the personal. I'm simply saying, our *feelings* are a barometer of how our *thoughts* are being utilized."

"Wow! This is remarkable," Janet exclaimed. "It's so different!"

"So what you're saying," Peter continued, "is that if people can learn to change their thoughts and forgive someone who has wronged them in the past, this will allow them to live without the heavy resentments they carried from those previous hurts?"

"That's about it," Andy nodded.

"Easier said than done," said Tom derisively. "What if you forgive someone for a malicious act and they do it to you again?"

With a very serious expression on his face, Andy replied, "Just because you forgive someone who has harmed you in the past doesn't mean you trust that they won't do it again."

"How can anyone just dismiss out of hand whatever experience is creating their problem with no assurance that the hurtful behavior will change?" Tom huffed.

Janet agreed, "It would be next to impossible for some people to forget all the ill feeling they have toward each other."

"You must remember," Andy told us, "you are forgiving the individual, not what he or she might have done to you."

Then he stood erect and, with the most loving smile on his face and a twinkle in his eyes,
said, "At least we can try. Forgiveness is the first
step. Please don't take me wrong. I'm not judging
you, your peers or anyone else. But may I humbly
suggest that you may be looking in the wrong
direction for your answers?"

"What do you mean by that?" Janet queried.

"Now, remember, Luv, I don't want you to get
your feathers ruffled by what I'm about to say. I am
not judging anyone—this is only my personal
observation."

"We won't get our feathers ruffled or our
noses out of joint," Janet replied with a laugh.

"In that case," Andy said, "may I propose this
to you? At times your profession appears to concentrate on mental illness more than it does on
mental health. It seems concerned more with the
negative than the positive."

"You've got to explain that statement, Andy,"
I said.

"The way I see it, Eric, the secret to mental
well-being doesn't lie in the past. It lies in the present or what many philosophies refer to as *the now*.
What you have to realize is:

> *The power of Thought is one of the*
> *most primal force functions of all*
> *human beings. Without it, there is*
> *no way we could experience life."*

"Don't you see Peter?" Andy continued. "One of the strongest antibiotics to heal the soul and help purify your mind is *forgiveness*. It assists the mind in returning to purity of *Original Thought*, where the peace and wisdom you seek lies."

For the longest time nobody said a word. I finally broke into the quiet by asking Andy for his definition of mental health.

He replied, "I imagine you doctors have a way of defining mental health that is altogether different from my personal idea, but I would define it this way:

> *When mind and soul are in unison,*
> *you will experience mental*
> *well-being."*

Both Peter and Janet laughed, saying Andy's answer wasn't exactly what they had expected.

"Yesterday you mentioned consciousness to us," Tom interjected. "How can anyone possibly explain consciousness?"

"They can't explain it," said Andy. "*Universal Consciousness* just is."

"That's not much of an answer," Tom complained.

Andy thought for a minute. "Well, you could say *Universal Consciousness* is the *power* that enables us to experience reality, and the purer our thoughts are, the higher the state of *consciousness* we live in."

Peter said he was taught there were different types of consciousness, such as male consciousness and female consciousness. He explained that many believe black people have a different consciousness than, say, Hispanics or Orientals.

Andy shook his head slowly. "I can assure you, Peter, that whoever formulated such a theory was painfully mistaken. *Universal Consciousness* is the same for all living souls, whether they be black, white, yellow or somewhere in between. *Consciousness*, just like *Thought*, is a universal gift that has no form and is strictly impersonal."

Peter described the many consciousness-raising groups throughout the world, and said that Andy's theories on the subject were nothing new.

"That is perfectly true," Andy replied. "The things I discuss have been here on earth since day one. But now you have my mind just as curious as yours. Tell me, Peter, what do people look for in these consciousness-raising groups?"

"Oh, the group members look for little faults in their own characters and attempt to become better aware of them, or try to become aware of what is causing the problems in their marriages. In other words, they try to become consciously aware of what is happening in their lives."

Andy listened intently to Peter's explanation about consciousness-raising groups, then put two fingers over his lips as if deep in thought. "Correct me if I'm wrong, young man, but I think we're talking about two different things altogether. You

are talking about the *form* our level of consciousness has led us to, such as a bad marriage or an
unhappy life or whatever. However, I'm talking
about *Consciousness* as a spiritual, neutral power
before human experience."

Janet asked Andy if he could possibly explain
Consciousness in another way. Andy threw his hands
into the air. "I told you it couldn't be explained," he
said with a boyish smile. "But I'll try."

After a brief pause, the gardener continued.
"Consciousness is one of the three principles of
human life. It is a precious gift we have been
blessed with that gives us the ability to realize the
existence of creation, to relate to each other, and
to fathom this great mystical world we live in.

"Did you know, Janet, there are an infinite
number of levels or states of consciousness? The
way we observe and react to reality as a whole
is directly related to the level of consciousness
from which we are functioning. Let me give you
an example: It's one of those days when you
wish you had stayed in bed. You're in a bad
mood and everything seems to go wrong. You
might even feel the entire world is against you
and, as far as you are concerned, it's someone
else's fault for making you feel that way. Of
course, when you have days like that, nothing
you do goes well.

"Now here is a strange thing: You go to bed
feeling awful. The next morning you wake up
and—lo and behold—you're in a better mood,

and you are relieved to realize the whole world isn't against you after all.

"Now, think about it, Janet—the world hasn't changed. It's the same old world out there; what has changed is your *level of consciousness*, which has come back to a more logical state, enabling you to see life with more clarity and understanding.

"It is very important to remember that the gift of *Consciousness* has no form or power of its own; how you use it is strictly up to you. This gift gives us the ability to recognize that there are different levels of existence.

"The way I see it, levels of *Consciousness* are similar to an outside elevator on a tall building. It goes up and it goes down all day, every day. The higher the elevator car ascends, the more can be surveyed. Views that may be blocked from the fourth floor can easily be seen from the tenth.

"Similarly, the higher your level of consciousness, the more understanding will be in your heart. The higher the consciousness elevator ascends, the more you see and understand, allowing you access to more common sense and wisdom. That is, when your consciousness ascends to a higher level, it assists you to see beyond whatever misled thoughts were obscuring your vision yesterday.

"Now consider that if someone were trying to explain such a psychological elevator ride—say, to the twelfth floor—to a person who had never been above the second floor, the conversation would appear mystical for the simple reason that they would be talking about the as yet unknown.

"I tell you, Eric, you can try to analyze or explain *Consciousness* forever and you will never achieve your goal—guaranteed! If you continue to try to analyze *Consciousness*, you will never come to the end of your futile journey. The important thing is, now that you know Consciousness exists, forget trying to analyze it and simply *use* it.

"You know, it's amazing how many people in this world search in vain for the knowledge that will aid in their understanding of Consciousness. It has been my observation that they fail because they look *outside* for the knowledge they seek instead of looking *within* for the innate knowledge that lies deep within their own consciousness. Remember, friends, you are looking for *wisdom*—and wisdom is knowledge before the contamination of human thought.

"This is the true definition of a mystic: Someone who deals in wisdom. Such people talk before time, space or matter—what I call the impersonal. But because they are speaking to people like you and me, they have no choice but to use words. They use metaphors and similes. Perhaps someday, if you can learn to listen, you will hear beyond the word to what the metaphors truly mean."

"Wow! That's quite a statement," Janet remarked.

"Trust me, Janet," Andy said gravely, "no matter how clever or knowledgeable a speaker you are listening to, their words alone can never give you the answers you seek."

"Then how can we find those answers?" Peter retorted.

"There are wise mystical writings all over the world; you can find them in libraries, bookstores, schools, churches. Truth is everywhere—if you can see it. But you have to remember that the words of the wise can only take you so far. Then it's up to you to go beyond their words to their *true* meaning— because what you seek has no form and words are only a representation of inner knowledge. Only you have the power to unlock such wisdom."

I asked Andy for his definition of life. He scattered the last of his fish food over the surface of the pond before replying, "I would define life this way:

> *Life as we know it is a*
> *divine dream*
> *Suspended within the boundaries*
> *of time, space and matter."*

"Why do you say that?" I asked.

Andy sighed heavily. "Because that's the way I see it—and I can't possibly explain to you why I see life the way I do an any more than you can explain to me why you see life the way *you* do.

"We all live in separate realities, but although we all see and react to life differently, we all use the same three gifts: *Mind, Consciousness* and *Thought*.

We use them in our own way to suit our own personal way of thinking. But regardless of how we may be separated by personal thought, we are all tethered together by the spiritual trio: *Mind*, *Consciousness* and *Thought*. They hold the secret of the form and the formless being one."

"Andy, I don't quite understand what you just said regarding form and formlessness being one," I admitted. "Could you approach that from another angle?"

"Okay, Eric, let's put it this way: Every cell in this majestic universe is created from the same formless, spiritual energy and cannot be separated from the whole. When this formless energy takes on a form, we call it the physical reality of time, space and matter. However, in essence both the form and the formless are the same energy in a different disguise.

"This is what is sometimes referred to as the *Oneness* of life—when the form and the formless are seen as one. Remember,

> *Everything is One Divine Cell,*
> *which is the main*
> *building block of this physical*
> *world we live in.*"

Showing intense interest and barely giving Andy a chance to finish, Janet asked him, "Why do you say that everything is the same formless spiritual energy and only differs in the form?"

"Luv, it's beyond my capabilities to explain that to you—but if you want me to put my two pennies' worth in and point out a few little things, I'd be honored. But let me suggest that you be careful not to get my finger confused with what it's pointing at.

"What if I were to tell you nothing can escape from this world? The simple reason is that everything is created from the same formless spiritual energy. Every grain of sand, every atom of matter, air, fire and water, everything in this universe is the same energy in a different disguise."

Pointing to a pile of old leaves and branches, Andy said, "For example, if I burn that pile of old branches, I may destroy the physical shape of them, but the energy will always remain—however, that energy will now have taken on a new identity."

A rush of energy swept through me as I suddenly realized what Andy was talking about. "Are you talking about *Infinity*?"

"Yes I am. It's very wise of you, Eric, to notice that connection."

Looking puzzled, Janet announced, "I must be missing something here—what do you mean by infinity?"

I felt absolutely electrified as I explained to Janet, "When I was in India I had heard a few religious leaders and mystics say, 'There is no beginning and no end to life,' but I never really understood what they meant. Just now I had a deeper appreciation of what the mystics in India were really saying. Just think about it, Janet. If everything is *One Divine Cell*, there couldn't possibly be a beginning or end to the *same energy*."

Peter shook his head, looked first at Janet then at me. "Eric, what you just said about infinity can't be proven one way or the other—it's strictly your personal opinion. It's common knowledge that the scientific field has been trying to prove whether or not there even *is* such a thing as infinity."

Ignoring Peter's comments, I told Andy that what he had just said had blown my mind. "This is unbelievable. It's so simple! You know, Andy, up until just now I always thought *Infinity* started in the present, instead of realizing that there couldn't possibly be a beginning to *Infinity*, could there? I can't believe I didn't see it before now."

Andy, smiling an enormous smile, made no reply.

Looking over at Janet, I could see she was struggling to comprehend the basis for my excitement. She shook her head and muttered, "I'm sorry Eric, but I just don't get it."

It became obvious to me as Janet continued her struggle to understand that I couldn't begin to explain my own insight. I realized that even as I spoke, the flash of understanding I had felt was fast disappearing from my head—into oblivion. But whatever I had experienced left me with the most incredible feeling of elation and wonder as I continued thinking about *Infinity*.

I indicated that I wanted Andy to continue the discussion of his theory that everything was the same energy—and of that energy's relationship to infinity.

Pointing to his head, Andy said, "Only in our little minds does the separation exist." Then, with another huge smile, he whispered, "I'm sure you must have heard the saying, 'We are what we seek'?"

"Many times," I replied.

"Well that's another clue to the knowledge you seek, a clue to help you realize that there is no separation between what you seek and what you *are*. Remember, Eric,

> *The form and the formless together*
> *are Infinity in motion."*

With these words, Andy flashed another enormous smile, stood up and thanked us for an interesting conversation. He then walked away, leaving us to contemplate his philosophical ideas regarding everything being one and my own realization that he had been talking about *Infinity*.

We sat for some time, turning Andy's last words over in our heads. Then, at Janet's suggestion, we walked to the village in search of a cup of coffee. The conversation quickly drifted toward a discussion of the gardener's obviously fervent belief in the importance and validity of the three principles of *Mind*, *Consciousness* and *Thought*. On the way back to the hotel, Tom spotted the gardener sitting on one of a pair of gnarled, bentwood benches and immediately headed toward him.

Andy greeted us with his usual smile. "Good afternoon! How are you doctors enjoying yourselves?"

"Very well, thanks," Janet replied. "We've had a wonderful day so far. We certainly enjoyed our conversation with you today. I know I found it very interesting."

Tom, on the other hand, couldn't resist challenging Andy. He declared that he couldn't accept the validity of the three principles. "In fact," he fumed, "should we give them any credence at all? If there was any validity to what you're proposing, if your theory regarding the principles you talk about were true, there would have been intensive studies done by now. Why haven't there been any field trials in psychology that investigate this?"

"I haven't the slightest idea, Tom," Andy replied. "Perhaps there have been and you just aren't aware of it. How should I know? I'm just a gardener."

Peter said, "I still don't quite see how these three so-called powers fit into the picture of mental health, or why you think we should place such importance on them."

Andy invited us to join him, then paused long enough to pour himself a cup of tea from an insulated bottle he produced from his lunch kit. Finally he said, "Peter, it's been my experience in life that the quality of my mental well-being is determined by how I use these three precious gifts."

Peter's inquisitive mind still couldn't stop formulating questions. "Why do you place so much emphasis on *Thought*?"

Andy's reply to Peter's question surprised us all:

> *"Thought is the spiritual catalyst*
> *that springs*
> *Mind into action and*
> *produces form."*

"*Thought* is the master key," he continued. "It can keep you a prisoner of your past or it can set you free."

Tom, being an atheist, naturally resented any of Andy's answers that alluded to the spiritual or to a soul, so he asked, "What's the 'soul' got to do with mental health?"

An expression of shock crossed Andy's face. Then he explained to Tom that, as far as he was concerned, the soul and the psyche were one and the same. "Just two different names for the same thing," he asserted.

"I've never heard that connection before," Tom snapped. "I don't see what the so-called soul has to do with psychology."

Before Andy could reply, Peter said he still remembered at least part of the *Oxford Dictionary*'s definition of psychology. "I believe it was something like, 'Psychology: The science of nature, functions, and phenomena of the human mind (formerly also the soul).'"

I had to confess that, like Tom, I thought the concept of a soul had more to do with religion or philosophy than with psychology.

"Me, too," remarked Janet. "As a matter of fact, I never heard anyone discuss a link between soul and mind in all the years I attended school."

Andy further surprised us when he said, "All I can tell you is that when the lot of you stopped your investigation into the connection between *Mind* and *Soul*, you threw away one of the most important clues to your investigation into the mysteries of mental health."

"What you have to try to realize," he continued, "is that such knowledge is found only when human thoughts transcend the intellect, reaching a realm beyond, deep in the soul, where the end of the rainbow and the divine pot of gold truly exist. This is how you will find elusive wisdom, not by delving into the past."

His words were said in such an authoritative voice that we couldn't protest. Not even Peter, with his fierce intellectual inquisitiveness, could ask any more questions.

Chapter 12

Acquiring Wisdom

*F*or a while I sat deep in thought. I snapped out of my reverie to hear Andy saying, "I can't imagine why you people don't look for plain, old-fashioned common sense. Seek the *logic* of the psyche, or the *Psycho-Logical*." The gardener grinned impishly at his own play on words.

I had the distinct feeling that Andy was baiting someone to challenge him—and that someone wasn't going to be me! It was Peter who bit, of course. He made it very clear to Andy that there were many in this world who would resent the idea that there was a difference between their intellect and wisdom.

"Perhaps there are," Andy replied. "But I'm afraid that's not my problem. We just have different opinions about life. Believe me, Peter, if I have ever upset anyone with my statements, I apologize. I can assure you it is unintentional and I'm certainly not putting down the intellect. As a matter of fact, I wish I had as much intelligence as you doctors have."

Peter, proud of his intellect, asked Andy once again, "What then, in your opinion, is the difference between what you call wisdom and the intellect?"

Without any hesitation Andy responded, "The way I see it Peter, wisdom is an inborn spiritual knowledge that lies deep within the soul of all human beings. On the other hand, intellect is just our capacity for learned and memorized knowledge. One could say the ego and our intellect are functions of our personal mind, while *wisdom* is a function of the spirit."

Janet asked Andy if he would elaborate on the difference between the two.

The gardener considered for a few seconds, scratched his head, then said, "Being therapists, you could say that *wisdom* lies deep within your psyche and that such knowledge is revealed from the inside out. *Wisdom* is an innate God-given intelligence, before the contamination of any personal thoughts. Intellectual knowledge, on the other hand, comes in from the outside world— the outside world being nature and everything you survey."

"You've lost me somewhere," Peter declared. "What do you mean by wisdom comes from the *inside out* and intellect is acquired from the *outside in*?"

Andy replied, "I have already explained to you that wisdom lies in the soul of all human beings. This is why I say to you, wisdom is revealed from the inside out."

For the longest time, no one said a word as we all tried to understand Andy's unique philosophy.

Something Andy said had intrigued me, so I asked him to explain what he meant by "before any *personal* thoughts."

Andy contemplated for a little while, then replied. "This physical life, all matter and all that we can survey, is what I am calling *after* form. That includes all personally formed thoughts, or, if you wish, your intellect."

I asked Andy what he meant by the term "*contamination* of personal thought."

Once more Andy sat quietly for a few moments as he carefully considered his answer. Then he said, "Before personal thoughts lie the virgin spiritual thoughts sometimes known as *wisdom*. Or similarly, before personal bias can affect thinking, there is *original thought*."

Andy waited to see if anyone was going to challenge him, but no one did. He continued, "The fortunate ones of this world have found a balance between their inner wisdom and their *personal intellect*."

We must have looked baffled. Smiling, Andy explained, "This is why we can have *The Nutty Professor* or the wise teacher. One has wisdom accompanying his intelligence and the other hasn't. When wisdom is lacking, our intelligence can, ironically, be our own downfall."

"What do you mean by that statement?" Peter inquired. "Can you give us an example?"

Andy stood up. "Take Hitler, for example," he said. "The way he manipulated the whole German nation and many others to get his own way was definitely shrewd and *intellectually* cunning, but he was completely out of touch with his own inner wisdom and was quite mad, making him a very dangerous person."

"There's no argument there," Janet replied. "But how do you suggest we find this inner wisdom?"

"My dear young lady, there are many ways to find such knowledge, which is why we all must exercise our own judgment and follow our own hearts when seeking such answers. But I guarantee you one thing: Regardless of how you may search for it, such a treasure will always be found from within the depths of your own consciousness."

"I'm with Janet," Peter remarked. "I'd like to know how you find such knowledge. To date, I think I've read over a thousand books and I still haven't found what I'm looking for."

In the most compassionate voice, but with a twinkle in his eye, Andy pointed to a butterfly on a nearby bush and said, "I am told one of the main criteria to find such knowledge is to:

Let your mind be still,
for the wisdom you seek is like that
butterfly over yonder.
If you try to catch it with
your intellect,
it will simply fly away.
On the other hand, if you can still
your mind,
someday, when you least expect it,
it will land in the palm of
your hand."

Although he appeared deep in thought, a responsive smile lit Peter's face as he considered Andy's answer.

After a lengthy silence, I told Andy that some of the teachers I'd met in India had used words very similar to his. "The only difference was, I never heard them discuss the subjects of *Thought* or *Consciousness*," I said. "Many of them, however, talked about little mind and Big Mind, but nobody ever really explained their connection to each other."

"Perhaps they would have, if they had known you and your friend were training to be therapists," Andy chuckled. "Then again, maybe they did offer the explanations, and you just weren't ready at that time to appreciate what they were trying to bestow upon you."

"Possibly," I replied. "Although, I remember there was one particular mystic I met in Nepal who was a very unusual character. He was a little, skinny guy with shiny, coal-black hair that hung all the way down to his waist. I remember he had an extraordinarily serene face and his deep brown eyes were so gentle looking; there was something about him that made you think, 'this man knows what he's talking about.'"

"What was so different about him?" Peter asked.

"It's really difficult to explain," I said. "I just remember that he talked in quite a different manner from all the others I'd encountered on my travels."

"But how was he different? Can't you explain what you just said in a little more detail?" Peter queried.

"Well, although this individual spoke in a highly mystical manner, he always answered questions in a non-prohibitive way. He was always non-judgmental. But to be truthful, I don't really remember too much of what he actually said; it was more of a feeling that emanated from him than any intellectual understanding. One thing I do remember is that he talked about our time in the world being *a divine mystical journey*, and throughout my travels he was the only one I ever heard speak in such a fashion."

Andy and my three colleagues sat quietly listening to my story. When I finished, Janet wanted to know what else was different about what this particular Nepalese mystic had to say.

"I tell you, Janet, he really confused my friend and me when he talked about the world being connected to the great nothingness."

Peter looked quizzical. "What did he mean by 'the great nothingness'? How can there possibly be a *great nothingness*?"

"I haven't the slightest idea," I answered. "As I said before, I understood very little of what the man said. However, he did say that if we could understand the riddle of the *great nothingness* and the *allness* being the same, we would find our answer."

The three other therapists sat speechless, then burst into laughter at such a conundrum, wondering what the mystic could possibly have meant by such a paradoxical statement. Then, with measured sarcasm, Tom asked Andy what he thought about the mystic's views on nothingness.

"Nothing," Andy replied playfully. Then, with a more serious face, he said, "It seems to me that when Eric was in the Far East, he may have had the good fortune to stumble upon someone who knew what he was talking about."

With a look of disbelief, Janet asked Andy, "Are you trying to tell us that you have some idea what the mystic meant when he talked about the *great nothingness* and the *allness* being the same?"

Andy shrugged his shoulders and, in the most casual way, replied, "The way I see it, Luv, the *great nothingness* is the spiritual reality *before* form; the *allness* is spiritual reality and physical reality as a whole, which includes the form and formless. Such a concept can most definitely only be found within the depths of your own soul. After all, how can anyone tell you about *nothingness*? That would be the equivalent of trying to eat the hole in the center of a doughnut."

We all smiled at Andy's answer. Then I recalled another thing the mystic had been quite emphatic about, and that was the importance of living in the *now*. "I remember a woman saying to the mystic that she failed to see how we have any other choice but to live in the now. 'We are here at this moment, are we not?' she asked quite defiantly."

"How did he answer her?" Janet inquired.

"I don't remember his complete answer, but I do remember part of it. He said, 'Yes madam, our bodies are here. But where are our minds?'"

"What did she say to that?" asked Peter.

"Not one single word," I replied. "I think she was probably as mystified as we are. I remember him saying something to the effect that, 'Living in the *now* is seeing *what is* instead of *what isn't*. And *what isn't* is created from living in the memories of the past and contaminating the *now*.' His answer was so unlike anything I'd been taught that I failed to discern any meaning in it."

With a large smile spreading over her face, Janet remarked, "That's quite the answer!"

"To be honest, Janet," I continued, "when I heard that mystic talk, I thought to myself, 'How could such answers help anyone?' Yet, that evening after we returned to the house where we were staying, my friend and I realized that we had never felt so energized in all our lives. Both of us remembered little—and understood even less—of what the man had said, but we agreed it was one of the most uplifting evenings of discussion on our entire journey. Again, it was the *feeling* more than an understanding."

"Did you ever speak with this mystic again?" Peter asked.

"No, I didn't," I sighed. "The next morning, my friend and I went back to listen to more of his spiritual and philosophical views, but he was gone. It was he who told me that if I had enough faith, someday I would find what I was looking for."

"Did he tell you where or how?" Janet asked.

"No," I admitted. "He just said he had the feeling that some day I would find what I was looking for. I remember as if it were yesterday... just before he left, he told those who were listening to him,

> *'Meditate and seek peace,*
> *for it is in the silent chambers of*
> *your mind*
> *that you will uncover the wisdom*
> *you seek.'*"

Chapter 13

Time to Reflect

$\mathcal{A}$fter Andy said his goodbyes, Janet said she had never in her life had such a conversation. "I feel so elated! It's like walking on air. But I also feel I need some time to myself to reflect on the old gardener's unique ideas."

"Me too," said Peter. "I feel the need for some quiet time. I want to think about what he's said regarding the difference between the intellect and what he was calling wisdom."

Tom adamantly declared that he already understood precisely what Andy was saying—and that the man was completely misinformed in almost everything he said. Tom further claimed that Andy was a classic case of an ignorant person talking far beyond his understanding.

As for myself, I honestly didn't know what to think. All I knew was that this was the first time I'd felt so elated since my meeting with the mystic in Nepal. Andy had that same special *something* about him. It's nothing you can point your finger to and say, this is what it is. But the way both Andy and the mystic answered questions with such assurance really impressed and fascinated me. Nevertheless, at that moment I felt just like Janet: I needed some quiet time to myself. We all agreed to spend the rest of the afternoon on our own, then meet up again later for dinner.

That afternoon I relaxed and took a stroll down by the river, thinking about some of our talks with the gardener. As I walked along the meandering footpath, I felt excited by the possibility that I may have found what I'd long been looking for. I thought about my wife, Norma, and longed to see her again so I could tell her all about our encounter with the unusual gardener. Every day, I thought how wonderful it would be to have Norma here so that we could experience the beauty of the English countryside together.

That evening during supper, my colleagues and I discussed what we had done during the afternoon. Janet said she spent most of the time in bed, having a good rest and thinking about some of the gardener's ideas. "The one that really got me was when he said, '*Going back into the past to fix yesterday's negative memories is like trying to blow out an electric light bulb.*' That statement really resonated with me," she said. "It just sounded so right."

Peter mentioned that he, too, had spent most of the afternoon lying down, mulling over some of the old gardener's unique beliefs. With a smile, he added, "Especially the ones that annoyed me. What really bothered me the most was how absolutely certain Andy appeared to be about his philosophical views."

Janet asked Peter whether he really believed it would make any difference if Andy showed any doubts about what he was saying.

"Yes," Peter said with a self-conscious laugh. "I instinctively mistrust people who are so sure of themselves."

Looking down her nose, Janet smiled at Peter. "So what you are saying is that you would rather listen to someone who isn't at all sure of what they are talking about?"

Peter, waving his finger at Janet, said, "That's sneaky, Janet." But he had a good laugh at the trap she had lured him into.

After a lengthy silence, Janet remarked, "Who would have thought before we left the States that we would be so affected by a series of fascinating conversations with an old English gardener?" She then changed the subject by saying, "Eric, the transformation in your patient, Mrs. Taylor, was remarkable—and whatever she saw might hold at least part of the answer to the riddle that we're all trying to solve. I'd love to talk to her and ask her what she heard and experienced that changed her life so much."

"Me, too," said Peter. "Since hearing her story, I've become absolutely captivated by the whole episode. I tell you, Eric, if I'd heard this story from anyone else, I wouldn't have believed it. It still seems a little far-fetched, but if it is true, that kind of story could give new hope to millions of people who have all but given up in sheer despair."

"As I told you before, Peter, this is one of the reasons my practice has taken off like a rocket," I said. "Mrs. Taylor has been spreading *hope* to some of her friends. The most remarkable thing is that many who start to understand there is a relationship between their thoughts and how they feel from day to day are responding in a way I've never seen before. It doesn't seem to matter who or what they are. As soon as they connect their own thoughts to their way of seeing life, they just seem to change. I tell you, I haven't seen so many rocky marriages being healed in all my life."

At this point, the waiter announced that the evening meal was a buffet and asked us to help ourselves whenever we were ready. The spread was enormous, with hot and cold regional favorites as well as beautifully prepared international dishes. We exclaimed over the roasts of lamb and beef, the cleverly presented poultry and colorful vegetables, the appetizing array of savories, and promised to leave room for the truly decadent desserts, many of which were served with clotted cream.

After we had made our choices and settled ourselves back at the table, Janet said, "You know, Eric, after you told me about Mrs. Taylor, and what you said about her thoughts having a lot to do with her recovery, I started to think about a couple that came to me for counseling. They had been married for 10 years and had three wonderful children, but the husband felt there was something missing in their marriage. He also felt that he had lost his one and only true love before he met his wife. The wife felt her husband didn't love her any more because he constantly talked about the girl he had been engaged to as a young man in college.

"Although he said he loved his wife, the man just couldn't get his old girlfriend out of his mind. When he thought about this old girlfriend, he would withdraw from his wife and family with absurd ideas in his head about being married to 'second best.' Of course, their children were drawn into the unpleasantness. It was as if this man was blind, and for the life of me I couldn't understand his mentality. Regardless of how I tried to get him to recognize how much his adolescent crush on a now nonexistent teenager was ruining his marriage, he just couldn't see what he was doing to his family."

Peter commented, "That must have been an awful situation for his wife."

"It was one of the main reasons she came to see me," Janet agreed. "She had given up hope that their marriage would last much longer."

"What was the final outcome?" I asked.

"Shortly after they came to see me, her husband received an invitation to attend the 20th reunion of his graduating class. Needless to say, his wife was not thrilled, because her husband's old girlfriend would also be attending. Of course, you couldn't blame the poor woman one bit. I can only imagine what bleak emotions she must have experienced. She must have gone through hell.

"Although my client didn't realize it at the time, this was the turning point of her marriage. Apparently the husband got the shock of his life when he met his old sweetheart. She wasn't anything like he had remembered! And, although she was still a striking woman, she had turned out to be an obnoxious and overbearing boor who barely remembered him and seemed to enjoy making tasteless jokes at other people's expense.

"Returning home, my client's husband finally realized just how lucky he was to have such a faithful, loving and caring wife and such beautiful children. From then on, their marriage soared. To be sure, the marriage was being ruined by his *thoughts* of a long-gone romance that he only *remembered* as wonderful. I honestly never thought about this case again until I heard you talk about the power of *Thought* and the experiences Mrs. Taylor went through," Janet concluded.

Nodding, Peter said, "The more we discuss this *Thought* concept, the more intriguing it becomes. As a matter of fact, I think I could dig up a few examples myself, cases where my clients' thoughts have led them astray. When I get back home, it's going to be very interesting to investigate this phenomenon in more detail. I don't imagine this thought theory fits every case, but I suspect it may fill the prescription for quite a few people."

"I'm not swallowing all that nonsense the old gardener is peddling about thoughts," Tom snapped. "You people are deluding yourselves, and that old guy really bothers me."

Janet couldn't resist commenting, "Perhaps you're afraid that he knows something you don't."

"That's total nonsense," Tom snarled.

"Then why did you want to talk to the old gardener in the first place, if you didn't have at least a glimmer of hope that maybe he knew something worthwhile?" Janet queried.

"Sheer curiosity," Tom huffed. "Sheer curiosity."

Janet smiled. "Um-hmm!"

Chapter 14

The Illusionary Ego

The following morning, after a hearty English breakfast, Tom was going sightseeing at Warwick Castle with a couple of the other practitioners attending the conference, so Janet, Peter and I decided to look around the nearby hamlet of Bourton-on-the-Water.

When we arrived at the village, Janet displayed an abundance of enthusiasm, more than enough for all three of us put together. She continually exclaimed how exciting it was to be in a village that was so ancient. "Imagine," she would say, "we are walking around in a place that is so much older than the United States" and "just look at those gorgeous old stone buildings" and "I can't believe that some of the roofs are actually made of sliced stone" and "Isn't that view awe-inspiring?" Janet was typically a cheerful person, but I had never seen her quite so radiant and happy.

A gently flowing, stone-walled river ran through the town. Although shallow and narrow, the river supported a good-sized population of small fish and several different species of ducks. A group of children stood on the bank, having a wonderful time tossing feed to the birds. They squealed with delight as the ducks splashed back and forth, crowding to reach the latest offering of grain and upending to catch the food before it reached bottom.

We discovered that the stores, most of which were housed in beautiful old stone cottages, decidedly catered to tourists like ourselves. As we wandered from shop to shop, Janet found a few interesting things to buy for herself and for her parents, and of course we all collected a handful of the inevitable postcards.

Peter bought himself a flat, peaked English hat, which we were told was called a "caddie." All 6'2" of him strutted like a prize peacock, and he asked Janet again and again if he looked "English, pip, pip, and all that."

"Definitely," she replied and, with a lady-like curtsy, said, "Peter, if I didn't know any better, I'd take you for royalty. Apart from that, milord, you look positively handsome."

Beaming, Peter replied, "Wow! My ego just jumped up a few notches."

It was very obvious they were having just as good a time as I was. Peter's day was made complete when he found an antique car museum. For an absorbing three-quarters of an hour, we were taken back into the past by way of the automobiles and curios of days gone by.

After our tour of the museum, we found a charming little café, with outside tables, that had just opened for high tea. Sitting under a weeping willow tree, drinking tea and eating scones with clotted cream in such a picturesque English village, I had to pinch myself to see if I was dreaming. I couldn't imagine anything more delightful or restful.

Janet said there was no doubt in her mind that the tranquil feelings she was experiencing would fit Andy's definition of meditation.

The streets were packed with cars, and tourists milled about all over the town. Then, we were treated to an unexpected delight. Suddenly, from a little side lane, a herd of sheep, a shepherd and his two dogs appeared on the street in front of us. We wondered how the dogs could possibly control so many sheep under such difficult conditions. But control them they did, with such skill and agility that they were soon around the corner and out of sight without incident. It absolutely fascinated us. The thing that intrigued me most was the intelligence of the dogs. They obeyed every whistled command the shepherd gave, despite the many distractions of the tourist-filled town, and often used their own initiative to return a straying sheep to the flock.

By mid-afternoon the little town was host to every conceivable shape and size of person from all over the world; it was almost like attending a fashion show to see the splendid variety of clothing being worn by so many different types of people.

Like the United States, England in those days had its share of the people known as hippies, part of a youthful phenomenon that was spreading across the globe. While most people were content to accept the flower children as free spirits, Tom constantly grumbled about hippies, maintaining that the United States would collapse if some of these no-good, long-haired loafers didn't get jobs and help support the country. Like Tom, I was well beyond the age of most of these young people, but I found the whole movement very interesting and couldn't help but wonder about its worldwide development.

On the lawn fronting the river, some young people were dancing to the rhythm of guitars and flutes. Sometimes I secretly envied this younger generation the way they lived without constraints or inhibitions.

Abruptly, Peter's loud voice shattered the tranquil mood as he announced, "That old gardener sometimes worries me with his mysterious, cryptic statements. I can't help but feel he is either the biggest shooter of the bull I've ever met or one of the smartest men I've ever met. I honestly can't make up my mind which one I think it is."

Smiling, Janet suggested that when Peter got home he should start looking at reducing his ego or the hat he'd just bought might not fit for very long.

Just as she said those words we noticed an elderly couple approaching us. "It's Andy—and that must be his wife!" Janet said with great delight.

Peter groaned and said that he felt in his bones that he was doomed to keep running into and being confused by the old gardener wherever he went.

Janet knew Peter well and was aware that he was not too sure about Andy's philosophical views, so she feared her friend's outlook was creating a little one-sided rivalry.

"Now you behave yourself," she whispered to Peter. "Leave Andy alone, and don't even think of trying any of your professional tactics on that nice old man."

When he saw us, Andy flashed an infectious smile and asked us if we were having a good holiday.

"Absolutely marvelous," Janet replied. "This is the best conference I've ever attended and Bourton-on-the-Water is stunningly beautiful. It's *so* English."

Andy smiled at Janet's words and introduced his wife, Emily, to us. She was a slim lady who stood about 5'3" tall. Her head of beautiful gray hair, short, thick and glossy, crowned a girlish face with a tranquil appearance.

"Where is Tom today?" Andy asked.

I explained that Tom was touring Warwick Castle and that originally the four of us had planned to visit the castle later this evening. However, Tom had felt honored to be asked to accompany a couple of English doctors who knew a considerable amount about the castle's history, so of course he had accepted.

We invited Andy and Emily to join us for tea. After they sat down, we discussed the history and age of Bourton-on-the-Water.

As Janet had suspected, Peter couldn't resist starting a dialogue with Andy, bringing up the pros and cons of the workings of the ego.

Janet gave Peter a glance that clearly showed her annoyance at his trying to trap the poor gardener with such questions, especially in front of the older man's wife.

After Andy patiently and graciously listened to Peter's interpretation of what we therapists call ego, Peter sat looking smug, believing he had outfoxed the gardener with all the psychological ramifications of the terms *ego* and *id*.

However, Peter's smugness didn't last long. The boom fell when Andy answered, "The way I see it, Peter, ego is only a self-created, insatiable delusion invented by the personal mind."

Before any of us could answer, Andy continued, "Feeding one's ego is equivalent to someone's constantly eating chocolate to slim down. Both are unproductive patterns that cause self-inflicted wounds."

"I thought you said you knew nothing about ego, and now you are telling us that it's a non-existent entity! Isn't that rather presumptuous of you?" Peter demanded.

In a very soft tone, Andy replied, "I didn't say I knew nothing about ego. I said I didn't know how you, as therapists, define ego."

His metaphor of the chocolate seemed to hit a nerve with Peter, who immediately made it very clear that his ego was important to him. "If Tom were here," he added, "he would most definitely argue the point of whether or not the ego was important. For example, a person with low self-esteem and very little ego would definitely need a therapist's help."

"Oh, I see," said Andy. "Tell me, young man, is there any limit to how much you can pump up this ego of yours?"

"Well," said Peter cautiously, "you don't want too much ego or you are very apt to become egotistical."

As quick as a flash, Andy cocked his head to one side and trying, to hide the smile on his face, asked Peter, "You mean to tell me you can over-dose on ego?"

"Well, nobody likes someone who is too egotistical," Peter admitted sheepishly.

Openly smiling now, Andy said, "If anyone was asking my personal advice, I would say that instead of concentrating one's efforts on ego, one should *seek the Truth that lies within*. Ego and ego concepts change like the tide, whereas *Truth* never changes. Have you ever heard the expression, 'The truth shall set you free?'"

"Yes, I have," replied Peter. "But tell me,

Andy, what is your personal definition of *Truth*?"

Andy took out an old pocket watch from his vest pocket and looked at it for a few seconds, then gazed at Peter. "How can anybody explain *Truth*? *Truth* has no form; the second you try to put a form on it, it is no longer *Truth*. The paradoxical thing is, it is from this very *Universal Truth* that all things take shape."

"Can you explain exactly what you mean by *Universal Truth*?" I asked.

Andy looked at Emily as if to say, here we go again. Then he smiled and replied, "Since time began the wise have tried to explain their conception of *Truth* intellectually, knowing their words were no different from an artist's painting of a beautiful sunset. No matter how excellent the painting or how realistic the picture may appear, it is *not* the sunset. Similar to the artist's painting, the words of the wise have created only a *psychological illusion*."

"What do you mean by a psychological illusion?" Janet inquired.

"A psychological illusion is our personal interpretation of such knowledge," Andy replied. "The knowledge you seek can only be explained as a metaphor, for the simple reason that what you seek, owing to its spiritual nature, has no form."

"I understand that using metaphors makes complex concepts and deep knowledge more accessible," said Janet. "But I still fail to see what the spiritual has to do with the psychological."

The gardener answered her with the following words: "May I suggest to you, Luv, that if you want to find the source of your psychological nature, you must go beyond the physical to your *spiritual* nature."

"How do you suggest we do that?" Janet inquired.

"If you can find the true nature of **Mind**, it is here you will find the answers to many of your inquiries into the secret of human behavior."

Janet sat very quietly, as if she was in deep contemplation, trying to figure out Andy's unconventional ideas.

Peter asked Andy if he thought the mind and the brain were the same, or whether he saw them as altogether different.

Andy smiled, saying that Peter had more questions than there were stars in the sky. Then he continued, "The way I see it Peter, the mind and the brain are two entirely different entities. The brain is biological, whereas **Mind** is spiritual."

"I've never heard anyone explain mind and brain that way before," Peter admitted. "Would you care to elaborate on your theory?"

Pointing to his head, Andy explained that the brain by itself lacked the power to think; just as a refrigerator must have electricity to function, so the brain must have **Mind** as a power source to make it work.

Peter was surprised by this answer, but his intellectual curiosity was undiminished. It was obvious that he was enjoying his discussion with Andy and wanted to continue his debate. So, returning to his starting point, Peter said he wanted to talk more about ego. He asserted that Andy didn't understand the fact that his ego was important to him and that he'd lose his identity without it.

"You already lost your identity," Andy replied, "when you split yourself in half with an ego and an id. Believe me, young man, there is only *one true you*. In reality, ego is a delusion. Your true identity is beyond what you are calling ego or personality."

I asked Andy if he realized that his theories would eliminate most Freudian concepts of ego if they were adopted by our profession.

"Have you any idea what this would do to the field?" Peter inquired.

In a warm and compassionate voice, Andy said, "Yes, I think I have a good idea. Believe me, Peter, never in a million years will you find an answer to mental stability by investigating what you are calling the ego."

Janet looked over at Peter, waiting for his reply. When none came, she asked Andy, "What do you mean when you say our true identity is beyond the ego or personality."

"Our true identity is of a spiritual nature, and it is hidden in the very depths of each living soul on earth," Andy replied. "It is only the mortal minds of humanity that live in a duality with the illusionary ego."

Janet looked puzzled. "I realize this may sound a little odd," she said, "but at times I get a glimmer of what you are saying—just a quick flash. But the moment I try to think back to what you have said, that little flash completely vanishes."

Peter looked first at me, then at Janet, with complete bewilderment in his eyes, not knowing how to counter Andy's silence.

After a considerable period of silence, I said, "You know, Andy, when I was in India, I honestly never related what the Buddhists said about ego being a delusion to the Freudian ego I had been taught about at school. I have certainly never considered them to be the same ego seen from two different points of view."

Even as I said those words, I thought to myself, "Which one is most likely to be correct? On one hand we have an extraordinarily enlightened man, Buddha, saying ego is a delusion. On the other hand we have a physician and scholar, Dr. Freud, saying that ego is a reality. Which one is correct?"

Chapter 15

The Picnic

$\mathcal{A}$s the conference was drawing to an end, we were invited by Emily and Andy to join them on a picnic. After the morning session, as we'd agreed, Andy drove up to the hotel right on schedule. We four piled into our rental car and followed Andy to the picnic site. After a scenic drive that lasted about 20 minutes—over twisting country roads that occasionally afforded glimpses of delightful old manor houses, and lanes so narrow that we once had to back up and pull off the road for an oncoming car—we arrived at one of the most picturesque spots I'd ever seen.

Emily was waiting for us with some refreshing tea and lemonade. The place she and Andy had chosen was absolutely breathtaking. We sat beneath an old oak tree overlooking a farm Emily said was more than 600 years old; Andy figured the tree itself was at least 300 years old.

Sitting in silence for the longest time, we watched the sheep and cows grazing in the pastures below. How peaceful the English countryside appeared, especially when compared to the bustle of Denver's downtown traffic!

Janet offered to help Emily with the simple preparations, and after a while, they announced the food was ready and that we should all help ourselves. We continued to sit in silence, enjoying our lunch and admiring the beauty of our surroundings.

After a while, Andy asked Tom how he had enjoyed Warwick Castle. Tom very sheepishly admitted that, due to unforeseen circumstances, he and both his colleagues had instead visited the local pub and spent the rest of the day there. "We never did see the castle, but those three did," he said, pointing at Janet, Peter and me.

"Did you find the castle interesting?" Emily asked us.

Peter said that the three of us had thoroughly enjoyed ourselves and found the entire tour to be fascinating and informative. "You'll never believe this," he exclaimed. "The guide told us that, in some parts of England, if you were suspected of being a witch they'd hang you from a pole by your feet and dip you into the river time and time again. If you drowned, the church would apologize, your death having proved that you were not a witch, and give you a Christian burial. However, if you lived through the horrendous ordeal, that was proof, as far as they were concerned, that you were a witch. In that case, they would burn you at the stake. Talk about a catch-22 situation! Either way, as soon as they nabbed you, it was 'adios amigo.'"

We all smiled at the horrified expression on Janet's face as Peter was telling his story. Smiling, Emily looked over at Janet and said soothingly, "Don't worry, Luv, we no longer do those kinds of things. We've all become a bit more civilized."

A calming silence prevailed as we were again lulled by the beauty of the English countryside. We munched our sandwiches as contentedly as the black and white cows in the next paddock munched the grass.

The ever-curious Peter once again broke the tranquillity of the afternoon by asking Andy if he had any idea just how many books there were pertaining to the mental health field. "It makes it very difficult to choose who to believe or whose concepts to follow," Peter said.

"I imagine there must be countless thousands," Andy replied. "I guess all you can do is believe only what your heart feels is right. My advice is,

Let no one create your destiny."

"Agreed," I answered. "But how many times are we swayed one way or another, only to have to rectify our misunderstandings?"

Andy stood erect, stretching his back, and said, "I believe rectifying your mistakes is called getting experience, and I doubt if there's any end to the number of times you or I may have to do that.

"The way I see it," Andy continued, "*Followers* lose their God-given freedom of *Thought*, whereas *listeners* still maintain this precious gift because they are not tied into any one person's opinion or any one school of thought. Now, when you went to school, I'm sure you had a favorite teacher whom you admired, someone who helped and guided you when you really needed it."

"I remember just such a teacher," Janet said, "a Mrs. Horner. She taught algebra with an unyielding belief that none of her students should ever try to memorize her lectures, saying that her students should be trying to understand the principles *behind* what she was trying to convey. Throughout the entire semester, she would say with a very gracious manner, 'Memorizing this material may get you through your exam, but you will soon forget it. Do you know why? Because you won't understand the very *foundation* of algebra.' Then she would say, 'Only if you try to understand the *fundamental principles* will you understand my words; only then will the *logic* of algebra remain with you for the rest of your life.'"

"You had a very wise teacher," Andy said. "Now I am suggesting the very same thing as your teacher. You have to find and understand the *basic principles* of our psychological functioning if you want to get away from all the guesswork."

"Are you really suggesting," Tom snorted, "that these three basic principles of yours—*Mind*, *Conscious* and *Thought*—lead to the understanding of *all* psychological functions, just like the basic algebraic principles lead to the understanding of algebra?"

"Yes, that is what I am saying," Andy replied softly.

Once again, Andy's answer surprised the four of us. I knew for certain that none of my colleagues had ever had any training regarding such principles; we hadn't even heard of their existence. I couldn't imagine where Andy got such remarkable ideas.

"I don't now that I can agree with you on this," Peter said. "It's simply impossible to turn psychology into a science like algebra. There are too many variables!"

Tom's face turned bright red as he sputtered, "It is very obvious, Andy, that your oversimplification of this entire subject proves you don't understand the enormity of the number of determinants to human behavior."

Andy scratched his head and said, "My friends, what you have to understand is that the principles apply, regardless of the variables. After all, the variables are merely the principles in action."

Janet responded brightly, "Just like Mrs. Horner's principles in algebra!"

"That's correct, Luv, just like Mrs. Horner's principles in algebra."

With a surprised look on his face that was becoming something of a permanent fixture, Peter said he'd need a little time to think about Andy's last statement.

Janet asked Andy if she was understanding him correctly. "You maintain that all mental processes are linked somehow to the three spiritual gifts you talk about?"

"That is correct, Janet," Andy said with a warm smile. "And no matter what your creed or color may be, no matter what your station in life is, whether you be king or beggar, your personal perception of life is created through these three spiritual gifts: *Mind*, *Consciousness* and *Thought*."

"What makes you so sure that these principles exist?" Peter asked. "And if they do, how would psychology benefit from adopting such a theory?"

Andy smiled at his question. "I'm afraid you don't understand, young man. You don't adopt these powers. They simply exist, and they adopted both you and your psychology the second you were born."

Looking more and more puzzled, Peter said, "I just don't understand such a statement!"

Tom had been sitting very quietly for some time, listening to the conversations between Peter and Andy with great intensity. Then he asked why Andy thought there were only three principles. "Don't you think there might be more?"

"No, that's impossible," Andy said firmly. "They are the complete trinity of all human behavior and feelings. They are the spiritual powers that allow us to function as human beings in this physical reality."

After a lengthy silence, and now bubbling with enthusiasm, Janet asked Andy, "How do our five senses fit into the picture of the three principles?"

Andy asked for a few minutes to think about the question. At last he answered her. "The way I see it, Janet, is this: Our five senses—smelling, tasting, touching, hearing and seeing—are the tools nature gave us to assist in experiencing life. However, as important as they are, they are of no value unless they are activated by the spiritual trio—*Mind, Consciousness* and *Thought*."

Andy's words took me by surprise, just as they had taken Janet, and I most definitely needed some time to think about his answer. I had a profusion of unanswered questions buzzing around in my head, and I was quite sure the others did as well. I asked Andy why he put so much emphasis on the three principles.

"Because," he asserted, "*Mind, Consciousness* and *Thought* are the psychological trinity of all human experience on earth. *They are the hidden pearls that lead us to our true identity*."

Janet's eyes twinkled. She asked Andy to take a minute to explain a little more regarding the importance of learning about *Mind, Consciousness* and *Thought*."

Andy bowed his head as if in deep thought. "I'm afraid, Luv, there aren't enough minutes in a lifetime to explain that question. But I can tell you this: The investigation into the workings of the three principles is endless. What I know about how they work is very little, but I can assure you that one can never come to the end of learning their importance."

Tom asserted that Andy's statements were open for debate, and declared that he felt certain many in this world would disagree with the old gardener completely.

"I have no doubt there are many who would reject my ideas, Tom," Andy replied. "That is their prerogative. The very fact that they question what is being said proves my point. Whether they be pro or con, the very fact that they had to *think* in order to debate is my checkmate. When you think about it, Tom, we must have *Thought* to even think about discussing the matter. And if this is so, it is only logical that one would have to be *conscious* of the existence of one's own thoughts. This tells me that the two are inseparable; you can't have a thought without being conscious of the fact. *The two are one*. Again, it is only logical that in order to have a thought and be conscious of the thought, one must also have a mind. Once again, you cannot have one without the other; all three are inseparable. The trinity has been born *Mind*, *Consciousness* and *Thought*. All three are one."

A long silence followed Andy's interpretation of the three *Universal Constants*. Finally Janet said, "Andy, I'm sitting here listening to you, and I'm experiencing incredible thoughts and feelings, but I still don't truly comprehend what you are getting at."

The old gardener smiled at Janet. "I can assure you, Luv, that there are some things in this world that are unexplainable, and this is one of those things. When the puzzle of the three *Universal Constants* starts to make sense to you, you will know. Believe me, Luv, you will know. Those *feelings* you are talking about are the parcel *wisdom* comes wrapped up in."

Then Andy turned to Peter with an impish grin. "It won't come from here," he said, pointing to his head. "It will come from here." The gardener was now pointing to his heart.

"Wow! That is quite the statement, and it's definitely an unusual premise," Peter exclaimed.

After a long, thoughtful silence, I asked Andy, "Why did you state the other day that searching for psychological knowledge without blending it with spiritual knowledge would result in a cosmic lie, or at best a half-truth?"

I could see Andy searching for a way to put his explanation so that it would make sense to me. Then he said, "What you have to try to understand, Eric, is that your spiritual nature and your psychological nature are intertwined. The more they are harmonized, the better off you will be and the more you will understand life. I can assure you that separating the psychological from the spiritual is one-sided and provides only half the answer."

Janet asked Andy if he could explain in a little more detail his concept of the spiritual reality and the psychological reality being intertwined.

The old gardener dropped his head in thought again, then answered. "Remember, Luv, I'm speaking metaphorically. Imagine this big world being a pulsating ball of energy. Then slice it horizontally, perfectly in half. The bottom half you could call the physical side of life. The upper part of the ball you could call the spiritual world, and it is in the spiritual half where all the *wisdom* you seek is stored.

"The spiritual part of the ball is all-important. Without it, we would cease to have the power to *think*, or to learn the true nature both of ourselves and the world we live in. Keep in mind that the energy can move back and forth—the dividing line is one you have drawn arbitrarily, and it is like a permeable membrane, not a solid wall."

Emily smiled throughout the entire conversation, periodically glancing at her husband in the most loving way, as if she understood precisely what Andy was trying to convey.

Janet admitted that she still didn't get the connection between what Andy called spiritual knowledge and psychological knowledge.

"Me, too," said Peter. "I'm afraid you've lost me somewhere."

"I think you are trying too hard to figure it all out," Andy declared. "I told you the other day, such knowledge can't be grasped intellectually. It is something that has to be realized and uncovered from within your own consciousness. What you have to realize is that there's quite a difference between hearing *Truth* intellectually and getting it from a realization."

With growing excitement Janet replied, "What *is* the difference between realizing it intellectually and realizing it from within?"

Andy's eyes twinkled. "The difference is like night and day. One is a learned process from the physical world and the other is an inner virgin knowledge that lies deep within the consciousness of all human beings."

I asked Andy if he could give us an example. Without any hesitation he said, "Yes—Einstein! When Einstein realized his theory of relativity, it was a virgin thought—or, if you wish, an *original thought*. However, once he spoke of his finding it became *of this world*; it joined with his intellect and that of all humanity. To me, Einstein was both a wise *and* an intelligent man."

"How do we find such wisdom?" Janet asked. "You wouldn't believe the number of awareness groups I've attended, or the masses of books I've read in the search for some answers, both for myself and to assist in my work."

"Janet, there are many ways to try to find such knowledge," the gardener answered, "but it makes no difference which path you follow or which journey you take. You must first learn to *listen*; otherwise, no matter how anyone tries to explain the unexplainable to you, it will never make sense. You see, Janet, because the elusive knowledge you seek has no form, it can only be explained metaphorically—and until you learn to *listen*, you will only hear the metaphors.

"Now, I'm not talking about listening from the old noggin. I'm talking about listening to a little voice, deep within your very soul. This is the little voice that will take you to the knowledge you seek."

He continued, "Why do you think people meditate? Because meditation is good for the soul; it rests the weary travelers on their journey through life and cleanses the channels of their minds. The state of meditation quiets personal thoughts and takes you on a journey—past the illusionary ego and into the land of knowledge that lies within. This is where you will find the understanding you seek regarding the true mechanism of human behavior."

"Andy, I still don't get it," I admitted. "I've looked all over the world and, no matter where I've gone or how earnestly I've searched, I haven't found a satisfying answer. For one reason or another, there are always inconsistencies in the explanations I'm given. Could you possibly explain it another way?"

"All right, let's try it this way," Andy said with a wink. "Let me tell you a little story…

Once upon a time there was a very wise swami who was also a very ardent flute player. He would often sit for hours and play his meditative music. Then one day a young man came looking for some inner knowledge and asked the swami to teach him how to find the *Truth*.

The swami listened to the young man's pleas, then asked him to come back in 10 days for his answer. After 10 days had come and gone, the young man returned to the swami's house and waited patiently outside his door. Finally, the swami opened the door and invited the young man into his home.

'I have decided,' said the swami, 'to teach you to find the true wisdom that lies within.'

The young man was filled with pride when he heard that the wise Master had chosen him as a student.

'Your first lesson, young man, involves that little tree lying on the ground over there. I happen to know that the good Lord has hidden a very special flute inside it. I want to see if you can find that flute. If you can uncover it, I would surely love to see such a work of art.'

Using his Master's knife, the young man methodically chipped away at the tree in search of the elusive flute. Finally, after chipping at the tree for several days, the young man returned to the swami and said, 'Master! I have diligently cut and chipped the entire tree, and I can assure you there was no flute hidden inside.'

'Well done, my young apprentice,' the swami answered. 'You should be proud of your enthusiasm and hard work. But it is strange that one so diligent didn't find what he was looking for. I can't imagine the good Lord forgetting to put a special flute into that tree.'

After the apprentice had a day of rest, the swami asked to see him again. 'For your next assignment, I would like you to find a quiet spot and meditate on why the good Lord didn't put a flute in that tree.'

When the apprentice had meditated for two whole days, the Master again asked to see him. 'I would imagine, young man, that you have great things to tell me about the missing flute?'

'No, Master,' the student replied. 'I still don't understand why you are so convinced that there was a flute in that tree. Nor can I understand what this has to do with my finding the *Truth* I seek.'

The swami answered, 'Oh, but I'm absolutely certain that the flute was there. Perhaps, quite innocently, you may have chopped it up into goodness knows how many pieces without recognizing it for what it was. And as for the second part of your question, only *you* have the power to find the answer to such a riddle.'

The young student just couldn't comprehend the deeper meaning of the swami's words.

Finally the swami said, 'Young man, I've given great thought to your dilemma of not recognizing such a valuable flute. Therefore I shall assign you another task. This time I want you to go to the top of the mountain where tranquillity reigns. There you will find one more tree lying on the ground. This time I want you to take no knife, just enough food and water for three days. See if you can find the answer to the riddle of the missing flute.'

'But Master,' the student protested, 'how can I possibly find a flute without my knife?'

'Carve it in the silence of your mind,' the swami replied.

The young student, although bewildered by his Master's words and orders, did as he was asked. Three days went by, and the young student returned full of glee as he announced to the Master that he had solved the riddle of the elusive flute.

'Well,' asked the swami, 'what did you find on top of the mountain?'

'Master, for the first two days I felt confused by the orders you had given me. But on the third day it came to me like a flash of lightning—the flute I sought was there all the time, only it had not been carved yet. Then I realized that the *Truth* I seek is just like the flute and the tree—it lies within my soul, waiting to be exposed by chopping away all the unnecessary beliefs I have in my head.'

'Well done, young man,' the swami said with a smile. 'Well done.'

'But tell me, Master,' the student said, 'why did you send me on a wild goose chase when all you had to do was tell me the answer?'

'Young man, the important thing is that you realized the answer on your own. Had I merely given you the answer, it probably would have become just another of your beliefs.'"

Andy paused to let us absorb his story. Bewildered by the riddle of the missing flute, Peter questioned the gardener. "That's an interesting story, but I still don't quite see the connection to Eric's personal search for wisdom."

The gardener smiled. "My dear young man, perhaps you should all take heed of what happened to the young man in the story and try to find what you seek in the silence of your own minds. Just as the flute was hidden in the tree, the knowledge sought by each of you lies hidden in the depths of your own inner consciousness, waiting to be released and reshaped.

"May I suggest to you," Andy concluded, "that you take a look at your thoughts and chip away those which hide your elusive Inner Wisdom?"

I thought I had followed Andy's story but sought affirmation. "So what I hear you say, Andy, is that you believe mental health is already in us if we can detach the wrongful thoughts from our heads. This is definitely a new idea to me. I was trained to believe that mental health is taught—healing knowledge comes into your head from the outside. Now you are saying mental health comes to us from inside."

Andy studied my face for a while. "I thought you told me that, when you were in India, a few wise people told you to look *within* for the answer?"

"Yes, that's true," I said. "But that advice still confounds me."

Andy smiled. "I think you are trying too hard to fathom my words intellectually, so I will tell you again: It is not the words you seek, but the knowledge that lies beyond the words."

Still puzzled, I said, "You know, Andy, this may sound strange to you, but I don't understand that statement. I do on some mental level, but I have a hunch there's another level I don't yet comprehend."

Andy gave me a sympathetic look. "*Hearing*, as the mystics refer to it, takes you beyond the word to what the metaphor truly means. It is such knowledge that will set you free from the chains of yesterday, allowing you to see beyond the known to the unknown. Remember, Eric,

> *Only in the quiet chambers of your*
> *mind will you find real knowledge,*
> *for it is here—with the assistance*
> *of Mind, Consciousness and*
> *Thought—that the incubation*
> *takes place and the wisdom you*
> *seek is brought forth into this*
> *world of form."*.

Andy stood up and stretched. "I think I feel like a little walk. How about you, Emily?" Emily smiled, took his hand, and the two of them walked away, leaving us to our contemplations.

Chapter 16

A Prophecy

When Andy and Emily returned from their stroll, I was still trying desperately to comprehend Andy's baffling philosophical beliefs. One look at Janet, Peter and Tom told me that they were just as bewildered as I was.

Andy asked whether any of us would care to take a walk to the river's edge. Peter, Janet and Emily declined but, to my surprise, Tom accepted. Andy, Tom and I were soon enjoying a brisk hike.

On the way to the river, Tom mentioned that he used to be an avid fisherman and regretted that he hadn't brought his fishing gear. "Come to think of it, some of my best memories go back to when I used to fish. It always used to calm my old mind down."

"How long has it been since you last went fishing?" Andy queried.

"Oh, it must be at least 15 years now. I used to go with my son, Tom Junior."

"Did you enjoy fishing together?"

"At one time we both loved it," Tom said a bit sadly.

"Why did you stop?" Andy asked gently.

"Oh, lots of reasons, I guess. I got too busy at the office and couldn't afford to take the time off."

"Perhaps you should take your son out fishing again," Andy suggested. "Maybe that's where you will find that peace of mind you spoke of."

"You know, that's not too bad an idea," Tom conceded. "When I get home, I'll phone my son and see if he would like to go fishing. It's strange, Andy, but I've just been thinking, right now, I wonder what happened to my life and why it is that things are not what they used to be?"

I could tell that Tom's question was rhetorical; neither Andy nor I made any attempt to answer him. But I was truly amazed to see that the old gardener had somehow managed to reveal a more thoughtful and vulnerable side of my old colleague than I had seen in years.

We reached the river's edge and stood quietly, reflecting. Finally Tom seemed to be pulling himself out of his torpor.

"Do you have to buy a license to fish in the rivers in England?" I said to break the silence.

"Oh, yes!" Andy answered. "You definitely need a license. First you must buy a government license, although I have no idea what that costs. Then you have to pay the owner of the river a fee. Quite often you are allocated perhaps 100 feet or so of river to fish."

"Only 100 feet?" Tom gasped. "That's high-way robbery! You would never get away with that in the States."

"Remember, Tom," Andy said, "you are in England now, and most of our laws are older than your country."

"I realize that, Andy," Tom huffed, "but I still think it's a complete rip-off."

Andy burst into peals of laughter at Tom's righteous indignation over the local fishing regulations. After Andy's hilarity subsided, Tom became very serious again and started to confess how unhappy he was. He declared that his life was hell and that everything he touched these days seemed to go wrong. He couldn't understand why his life was in such turmoil. "As a matter of fact," he sighed, "just before I came on this trip, my associate informed me that he wants to dissolve our partnership. Apart from that, my marriage just came to an end."

"I'm truly sorry to hear that, Tom," Andy replied. "It must be an awful time for you. I have no doubt you are suffering from all the trials and tribulations you are going through."

"It hasn't been easy," Tom admitted. "When I get home I have an appointment with a friend of mine who specializes in such traumas, and I'm hoping that he can help me. To be truthful, Andy, I really don't understand what's happening to my life these days. Both my wife, or I should say my ex-wife, and my partner accuse me of being stubborn and unyielding. And if anybody was stubborn, it was my wife."

It was obvious to Andy that Tom was experiencing a considerable amount of pain. With great compassion, Andy said, "You know, Tom, I'm not saying you are stubborn, but it has been my experience that stubborn people can get themselves into a lot of trouble. One very important thing I've learned in this life is that happiness doesn't depend entirely on your circumstances but has more to do with how you *think* from moment to moment. Be careful what you do with your thoughts. Remember, if you pour water into a tea cup, it will take the shape of the tea cup. If you pour water into a bottle, it will take the shape of the bottle. Each one of us has to be like the water and be prepared to change with the mold life creates for us from day to day. But we must also be aware that our thoughts can profoundly influence the shape of that mold."

For a short while, Tom looked perplexed by Andy's analogies. "I think I know what you're getting at, but I honestly don't think I'm stubborn. Perhaps I stick to my principles, but that is a far cry from being stubborn."

With a knowing smile, Andy put his arm around Tom's shoulder. "Perhaps there are better days to come," he said brightly. "In the meantime, my friend, let's try to forget all our problems and enjoy what precious time you have left here in Jolly Olde England."

It didn't take long for Tom to forget his worries, at least temporarily, as he excitedly pointed to the passing trout. "Look at the size of that one," he exclaimed. "It must be at least 18 inches long! And look, there's another just as big. Maybe you *could* catch your limit in a 100-foot stretch of this stream after all!"

Leaving Andy and Tom to admire the fish, I wandered back to the picnic site and struck up a conversation with Emily and Janet. I described to Emily how I had met Andy a year ago and explained that we had talked quite briefly. I then told her that my own personal life had never been better and that my practice had changed dramatically.

Emily listened with great interest as I related the entire story of Mrs. Taylor's recovery and the results of some of my other clients who had picked up on the way their own thoughts shaped the way they saw life.

Emily didn't seem shocked or surprised by what I was saying. With a beautiful smile, she commented on how wonderful it must be to see such positive results in my work.

"It is," I replied. "At first, I didn't quite understand why I was getting such positive results; all I had done was talk to my clients about their thoughts. But as time went by, it became more obvious that my own thinking had a great bearing on *my* life, too. Then I started to realize that it was *universal*, and that everyone's behavior is somehow connected to how they survey life. Yet I could see there was so much more to learn! Since coming back to England and listening to Andy again, it's all starting to make even more sense to me."

Emily smiled. "You know, Eric, I have met many people, so many I couldn't begin to count them, who have found happiness beyond their wildest dreams, simply because they found the slightest glimmer of insight about how the power of *Thought* guides them through life."

Emily's face lit up, and she broke into a broad grin as she said, "What if I were to tell you that Andy has predicted that the '70s will bring about a new kind of therapy such as humanity has never seen before? He says it will be a psychology that will differ from most present-day concepts in that it will help individuals to realize the mental health they *already* have inside them."

"Wow! That's quite the prediction," I answered.

"I can't believe what I'm hearing," Janet declared. "Why did Andy say this new psychology will be so different from what is now practiced?"

Emily's eyes danced as she answered, "When I asked Andy that very question, he said, 'Because such a psychology will be *spiritually* based, and its healing powers will be beyond anything known to date.'" Janet smiled at Emily's words.

Emily said that Andy assured her that it was written and it would come to pass—and when it did, no one would be able to stop its progress because the new psychology would be renowned for its results.

Janet, astonished by Emily's words, asked her, "How can Andy know that such a prophecy will ever be fulfilled?"

"That, my dear young lady, I can't explain," Emily admitted. "But that's only half the story! Andy also maintains that even untrained people who understand what is being said will jump the boundaries of time and forge ahead of some of the archaic theories of today."

Janet said, "I'm getting those goosebumps again! This is almost like being in a fantasy movie where you never know what to expect next. Tell me, Emily, does Andy always talk in such a mystical manner?"

"I know what you mean, Janet," Emily said, "and the answer is no. Andy is a very quiet and private person, and he rarely talks to anyone the way he has been talking with you doctors. When I first met Andy, it took me quite a considerable time to realize just how deep his knowledge really was. Andy doesn't think like you or I. Believe me, Eric, what happened to you and your patients is nothing new. And I can assure you that Andy *does* know what he is talking about."

I told Emily how wonderful I felt about my work, and that a lot of thanks should go to Andy for sharing some of his philosophical views with me. "Each day I'm starting to realize more and more why Andy put so much emphasis on how we use our thoughts. Sometimes I'll find myself in the office when my whole mind seems to be in knots, just having one of those days when everything goes wrong. Then suddenly I'll realize that I have been allowing my own thoughts to create certain situations and bad feelings in my life, quite often needlessly. Since my last visit, this has happened to me quite a few times, and each time it happened it was like magic. My mind completely calmed down and I could quite clearly see the solution to my problem. This connection to *Thought* inspires me as a psychologist and brings life back into my work."

A beautiful smile spread across Emily's face as she said gently, "I hope you realize that Andy isn't talking about psychology as you do. He talks to you four doctors using the terminology and language of psychology only because he knows you are psychologists. If you listen very closely to what Andy is saying, you'll see that he always talks in the impersonal, and the impersonal suits every person on earth."

"What do you mean, Andy speaks of a different psychology than we do?" Janet asked.

"My dear, I just told you," Emily said with a soft laugh.

"Please tell me again," Janet urged.

Flinging her arms wide, palms upward in a gesture of mock helplessness, Emily replied, "My dear, you are asking a lot and I'm afraid it's beyond me to answer all of your questions. All I can suggest is that you listen to Andy very carefully, and you will see he isn't talking about personal truths and specific psychological problems as you may have been taught to do in your psychological training. Andy talks of a wisdom before the creation of what you call psychology or psychiatry, and what he says really has no connection to the beliefs of Freud or anyone else. He is speaking about another dimension of thought and psychology altogether. As a matter of fact, if you listen to him very carefully you will see that he is talking about a universal psychology that is both a cure and a prevention. I certainly couldn't begin to explain that to you!"

"That's quite the statement," Janet said. "But Emily, after living with Andy all these years, surely you must understand him pretty well by now."

"Pretty well," Emily acknowledged. "But what he knows and how he knows it is just as much a mystery to me as it is to you. In all our years together, I have learned many very beautiful things from Andy." There was a long pause, then looking straight into my eyes, she concluded, "All I can say is that our life together has been like a marvelous, mystical dream."

Janet said that during her entire profession as a marriage counselor she had never heard anyone describe their marriage quite as Emily had just done. "Emily, if you feel I'm getting too inquisitive, please just say so. But I'd love to know how you and Andy met."

Emily smiled. "Let me see... it was two years after the First World War, the spring of 1920 to be precise. I had moved to the outskirts of Torquay, in Devon, to take up the position of teacher at the local primary school. Andy was the handsome young manager of a farm called Heavenly Meadows. It was a happy place where all the employees were treated like one big family. He had his hands full keeping it running because of the shortages and the other problems brought about by the war. I had been teaching for about six months when Andy and I were introduced to each other at a friend's house one day, and that was it. We fell in love, four months later we were married, and here we are."

At this point, Tom and Andy returned from their walk and Janet asked if they had seen any fish.

"Yes," Tom said excitedly. "We saw quite a few beautiful trout, but you should hear the nonsense you have to go through just to get permission to fish in an English river. It's a complete rip-off!"

This set Andy on another round of laughter so infectious that we all joined in. It was several minutes before the laughter subsided as we joked and carried on boisterously about the size of the fish. Our hijinks even managed to wake up Peter, who had drifted off to sleep in the shade of the oak tree. Shaking off the last traces of his nap, Peter said, "Hey, I'd love to see those enormous trout."

   With that, Peter joined Tom and Andy, and the three of them wandered back down to the river's edge to have a look at the fish, leaving Emily, Janet and me to our conversation.

Chapter 17

About Love and Marriage

*A*fter Andy and the other two men had left, Emily told Janet and me, "My husband thinks both of you are very wise people. And believe me, Andy doesn't throw compliments like that around to just anyone."

Turning to Janet, she said, "Andy tells me you're a marriage counselor, and from what he said about you, I imagine you must be a very good one."

"I try my best," Janet said with a smile, "but like most people, I have my bad days along with my good. Perhaps if Andy knew me better he would reconsider his praises. Tell me, Emily, what is the secret to a good marriage in your opinion?"

Emily replied, "There really isn't any one secret. Andy and I were lucky; we found something very special in our lives, something that bound us together."

"I hope you don't mind my asking such questions," Janet blushed, "but it's so rare in my profession to find such a healthy marriage. What was this bond you found?"

Emily waited a few seconds before answering, then said, "Love and understanding."

"And what else?" Janet asked.

"Janet, I can't possibly answer such questions in just a few minutes," Emily protested good-naturedly.

"Well, do you and Andy ever disagree?" Janet asked.

"Of course we do," Emily replied. "We're only human, and no one is perfect."

"Except you and me," Janet quipped, her eyes twinkling.

Emily immediately replied with a chuckle, "Of course! That goes without saying." Then she said, "Throughout the years, little by little, I have found a deeper understanding of life, which in turn brought more common sense into our marriage. Over time, Andy and I have found a lot of respect and love for each other. It's all a matter of sharing, loving and caring, never intentionally hurting your partner in any way. This is what I would call love, and this alone will create a healthy marriage.

"In marriage," Emily continued, "you must try to understand each other's little idiosyncrasies and forgive them. Just as Andy forgives me for any annoying habits I may have, I forgive him his. You shouldn't have to walk on eggshells, but you should try to be aware of your partner's sensitivities."

"What else goes into a good marriage?" I asked Emily.

"For a healthy marriage, I suggest couples should try to be each other's best friend. It's surprising how much trust and harmony it brings to a marriage when you realize your wife or your husband is truly your best friend."

"My big problem," Janet sighed, "is that by the time I get to see a couple in my office, there's usually almost zero trust for each other left. They're certainly not best friends at that point. And you wouldn't believe how many couples split up over trivialities. Before I met you and Andy, I often wondered if there were any good marriages left in this world."

"Of course there are," Emily said with a smile. "You must remember that in your profession you only hear about the marriages that have deep problems. But luckily there are still many healthy marriages out there with couples quietly going about their lives."

After a pause, Janet said, "You mentioned forgiveness being one of the main requirements for a healthy marriage. Would you mind if I asked you to explain in more detail?"

Emily sat down on the picnic table and invited Janet and me to sit beside her. Holding Janet's hand, she said, "My dear, sometimes forgiveness can go a long way to patch up an unfortunate wrongdoing. Sometimes it's the *only* thing that can."

Janet asked Emily what advice she would give a newlywed couple.

"I would tell them the very same as I have just told you," Emily said. Then, smiling brightly, she changed the subject, asking Janet whether she was heading straight home to America or if she was going to travel and do some sightseeing while in Britain.

"I have a wonderful vacation planned," Janet beamed. "After I leave here, I travel to York; I'm told it's a charming city, absolutely saturated with history. The travel agent also said that York's medieval city wall was constructed on top of an even earlier Roman wall, and the city itself is thought to cover a Viking ruin."

"You made a good choice," Emily remarked. "It is, as you just said, a little medieval city. Both Andy and I favor it highly; indeed, it is one of our preferred places to visit. If you enjoy antiques and antiquity, York will certainly fill the bill."

"I can't wait to see it," Janet said excitedly. "After I visit York, I'm flying to Ireland, where I have some distant relatives. My grandfather on my mother's side of the family came from Dublin, and I've always longed to see where he was born. I feel it's going to be marvelous to go back to my roots."

"What an adventure you have planned!" Emily said with a smile. "I hope you have a splendid time, and don't forget to send us a postcard from York."

Just then, the other three arrived back at the picnic site, all laughing at something Peter had said—something they would not disclose to the ladies.

It was nearing five o'clock, and Andy ended the day by saying that he and Emily should get home. He thanked us for joining them, saying how much he had enjoyed our talks and that he had found them very inspiring. Emily agreed it had been both a pleasure and an honor to meet us all, saying she had enjoyed the privilege of having such wonderful conversations with such interesting and important people.

Chapter 18

A Lesson in Shorthand

After Andy and Emily left, we lay in silence under the oak tree, gazing at the pastoral scene around us. I thought to myself, "No wonder people talk about the beauty of the English countryside. I guess the lushness is the pay-off for having so much rain." I was glad that we had been lucky and hadn't experienced any of the legendary English downpours so far.

I was experiencing the greatest feeling of tranquillity. I can't exactly express how I felt. It was as if all the stress had left my body and I enjoyed a wonderful peace of mind.

Janet said that she was feeling the same way, and that she wouldn't mind living in England for a couple of years to truly experience the English way of life.

Peter commented, "England certainly is a beautiful country, at least what I've seen of it. I'm like you, Janet—someday I'd love to come back and take at least two months to tour the whole of Britain. I'm glad I came to this conference, too. Without a doubt it's the best I've ever attended."

Then Peter changed the subject, asking me if I saw the old gardener look straight at him when he was talking about ego. "I tell you, it was the eeriest feeling. It was as if he knew my ego was bothering me."

"Come on, Peter, you're becoming paranoid," I said. "What makes you say that?"

"Because last night I realized that Andy has been saying things that I couldn't understand and, to be honest with you, it really bothered me when I realized my ego was not allowing me to listen to him. It's just so embarrassing to be told by a gardener about one's own profession."

"I feel for you," Janet said. "But you should have heard what Emily told us about a prophecy Andy has made."

"What prophecy?" Peter asked. "What did she say?"

Smiling impishly at Tom and Peter, Janet said that she didn't want to spoil their day and that she would tell them later.

"Come on Janet," Peter implored. "You can't just leave us hanging like that! What is this about a prophecy?"

"Well," replied Janet, "Emily told us that Andy predicts that there will arise in the '70s an all new psychological approach that will help millions of people."

Peter sat with a stunned look on his face, saying nothing for the longest time. "Wow!" he finally said. "That's quite the statement, even for old Andy. But how could he possibly know this to be true?"

Tears ran down Janet's cheeks as she said, "Whether we believe him or not, wouldn't it be wonderful if his prophecy *did* come true and we found even the smallest help for people?"

"Of course," Peter replied. "That goes without saying. What worries me is the fact that anyone can make such a prediction with such assurance. How can he be so sure before it happens?"

"I asked Emily that very same question, and she answered me by saying, 'Because he can *See*.'"

"What did she mean, 'Because he can see'?" Peter asked.

"I haven't the foggiest idea," Janet admitted. "When I asked Emily that question at the picnic site, she told me the following story: Some years ago, Andy and Emily we were relaxing under the old oak tree in their back yard, enjoying the softness of a summer evening. For some reason the topic of *Seeing* came up and Emily asked Andy to explain what he meant. He picked up an acorn that was lying on the lawn and, holding it up high, he said, 'Someday this acorn will look just like the oak tree we are sitting under. But it takes many years for it to grow and mature. However, if you can *See*, and you plant the proper seeds and jump the boundaries of time, the results of the planted seeds are apparent *now*.'"

"I really have no idea what you just said!" Peter exclaimed when he'd heard Janet's rendition of Emily's story.

"Join the club," I said with a chuckle. "I told you when we first came here that you might not understand much of what the gardener says."

Janet, wiping tears from her eyes, continued, "When I was in the 12th grade, I took shorthand. As you know, shorthand is written in symbols. Now you guys might think I'm crazy, but I'm pretty sure that what Andy is saying is only symbolic, and I'm positive he is talking in a form of shorthand."

Peter laughed and said Janet sounded like something from an Agatha Christie novel. Having a little fun with her, he continued, "And now, ladies and gentlemen, I ask you, does the old gardener talk in shorthand, or does he talk longhand?"

"Don't you see," Janet continued, ignoring Peter's facetious comments, "that this is why Andy doesn't want to get caught up in any unnecessary explanations to some of the trivial questions we have been asking him?"

At this point, I told Janet she must be perceiving something beyond what I was seeing.

"Me, too," said Peter. "I don't quite comprehend what you mean by Andy talking in shorthand."

Janet, in her own delightful way, appeared inspired. I'd never seen her so alive or excited as she said, "Shorthand is a series of small, quick strokes that represent something much larger, a sound or a whole word. Shorthand is only symbolic of what it really represents. As Andy himself said a couple of days ago, 'By its very nature, such knowledge can only be explained *symbolically* via the word.' This is why I feel he is telling us to find what we are looking for using a different approach than we would ordinarily."

Janet continued, "What I am saying is, while I don't understand his method of talking, I *am* getting the idea when Andy tells us to look at *Thought*, he is not telling us to look at our *personal* thoughts, nor is he judging what we do with them. What I hear him say is, there's a vast difference between the *power of Thought* and our *personal* thinking."

Peter thought for a while. "So what I hear you say is, we as therapists shouldn't concentrate so much on the contents of people's thoughts or what painful situations they may have created. Rather, we should concentrate on the *power of Thought*, which the old gardener so obviously believes in."

Tom and I laughed at Peter, saying he was starting to sound like Andy. Everyone immediately burst into laughter at that thought. Peter and Janet were laughing so hard that they were completely out of control. Even Tom managed a hearty guffaw.

I hadn't seen Tom laugh like that during the entire time I'd known him. After hearing about all the turmoil he was going through in his life, it truly was a joy to see him let his guard down and not be so serious.

Personally, I was astonished by how astute Janet was and how she appeared to comprehend more than any of us about what the gardener had been saying. As I mused over her explanations, I began to realize that Janet was understanding more in a few days than I had figured out in a year. At that moment I was filled to the brim with the most exhilarating feelings of well-being, and I knew in my heart that this weekend would live in my memory forever.

Chapter 19

Farewell

The following morning we woke to our first English downpour, the sheets of rain blowing this way and that, all but obliterating the view from our rooms. After breakfast, Peter and I checked out of the hotel and waited in the lounge for Janet and Tom. Finally, Janet appeared with arms full of luggage and parcels, apologizing for being late.

"Wow!" she exclaimed. "I've never seen rain like this before! When my alarm went off, it was still so dark out that I thought I must have set the clock wrong. I'm glad this weather waited until we were leaving. Oh, Tom said to tell you he'll be here shortly—he's just checking out. And speaking of Tom, I spent about an hour with him in the lounge last night and couldn't believe what I was hearing. I've never known him to be so positive! It was like talking with a different person, and he looks just great."

Peter added, "Something's happened to him, all right. Last night he suddenly announced to me that he wasn't going to take the three-day London tour with us as planned."

"Do you know why?" I asked.

"No, I don't," Peter answered. "But he was quite adamant about it and I couldn't persuade him to change his mind. He kept muttering something about, 'It's never too late.'"

At this point, Andy appeared to say his goodbyes to us. As he approached, I noticed a few weak streaks of sun beginning to mingle with the rain. Janet, more radiant than ever, immediately bid Andy good morning. She virtually bubbled as she said, "Thanks again to you and Emily for an unforgettable picnic. I truly appreciated the inspiring conversations with both of you." Handing Andy a little gift-wrapped parcel, Janet asked him to give it to Emily and to thank her for being such a wonderful hostess. "Please give her a special thanks for helping me to realize that there are good marriages out there, and for giving me great hope for the possibility of helping to strengthen even more of them." With tears in her eyes, Janet threw her arms around Andy's neck and kissed his cheek.

Peter stepped forward and shook Andy's hand. "I have to say that it has been a distinct pleasure meeting you, and I have very much enjoyed our intriguing conversations. Now, I'm not saying I agree with all of your philosophical views on life, but I have to admit that you've given me a lot to think about."

Tom stepped forward, shook Andy's hand and thanked him and Emily for their hospitality. Suddenly, looking very serious, Tom said, "That conversation down by the river yesterday made me look at something I've been avoiding for a long time." With these words, he again shook Andy's hand, then sped off to say farewell to some of the other therapists he'd met during the convention.

Finally, Andy turned to me. "Well, Eric, again we say our farewells. It was a pleasure meeting with you again and chatting with you and your friends. I'm glad to hear that your life is going so well."

With these words, he raised his cap, wished us all Godspeed on our journey through life, and left us to our last-minute preparations for the return trip. By then the rain had completely disappeared, leaving only glistening grass and trees and a few puddles on the driveway to show that it had ever been. Broad rays of sunlight burnished the clouds as they passed through the sky and began to warm the air.

While I watched, a stray beam illuminated the old gardener as he picked up the handles of his wheelbarrow and walked toward his beloved gardens.

The End